Change the World
Please !

Jack Stack

PRAISE FOR THE GREAT GAME OF BUSINESS®

"This book was a WOW factor for me. For outsiders it really shows that the Great Game of Business is so much more. This isn't just business changing; it's personal changing which leads to economic changing which leads to WORLD CHANGING. This is a movement of demanding more from ourselves, our leaders politically and professionally, and tributes so much for the next generation to demand happiness. Do people know they don't have to hate going to work? Seriously. There are companies who get it, who get you, who get that you have a family. You might have bad days anywhere you go but why are we so convinced that we have to settle when it comes to a job? How do we get everyone to know Great Game exists?"

—RINNIE REED

"From a cultural perspective, the Great Game of Business has given me a system that I can use to allow other people to flourish, be held accountable, and free up my time. It's been very enjoyable to see other people make great decisions because they have all the information, and they benefit personally from making a great decision for the company. From a business perspective, we are much more forward looking than we have ever been. Because we are continually forecasting, everyone in the company knows each week what our year-end profit expectations are. Early insight allows us many advantages in running our business. The Great Game is a beautiful system. It unifies our culture so that we all speak a common language, the language of numbers. Because of these factors, the Great Game of Business system has been very rewarding for me personally."

—DAVE VAN BELLE

"I can say with 100 percent honesty that I can attribute my success, the success of my businesses, and the impact I've been able to have on others in major part to what I learned practicing the Great Game of Business. I've had other opportunities to learn and grow since leaving SRC, but truthfully without the language of business to build upon, I know my trajectory would have looked very different. It's the universal language. The one that everyone should know, and the one that your organizations teach so well. Thank you for making it your mission to teach people business and for never ever wavering on that goal. It truly does and has changed millions of lives."

—KRISTIN BINFORD

"We all have dreams—typically big dreams—about what we want to accomplish in our lives or businesses and our organizations. Then we typically talk ourselves out of why we cannot make those dreams become a reality. This book allows people to dream big by showing them how many ways the Game can be adapted to every different type of organization. Every time I hear from someone that they are different, I can find a way that the Game would still work. I hope that this book and my story can provide that vision for all different types of organizations to see how it is possible. They deserve it, our communities deserve it, and most importantly, the populations served by nonprofits deserve the best. The Great Game allows organizations to operate at the highest level of efficiency while creating long-lasting sustainability. I hope this book inspires even more to realize they can play and win big."

—KATIE DAVIS

"Playing the Great Game of Business has certainly improved the financial position of the county. It has increased the level of financial literacy each team member achieves. It is also exciting to see that knowledge reach an individual's home finances, which directly effects the health of our community."

—CINDY STEIN

"The tools of the Great Game of Business have equipped me to not only grow my department's revenue 2,900 percent over the past sixteen years, but also to realize a dream come true for the Springfield Little Theatre education department, the purchase of a dedicated education facility, a dream 'factory' for emerging artists.

Working in theater, one might say that we are in the business of 'play.' As some of the hardest working 'players' on the field, the success that we have had due to the discipline of the Game, has inspired many other individuals, arts organizations and local non-profits to strive to model our success.

The principles of the game are so simple, but they've had a profound effect on my life and the lives of our staff, our volunteers, and our students, creating a culture of teamwork, accountability, trust, ingenuity, and perseverance. We are in it to win it!

No money, no mission! I will be forever indebted to Jack and Betsy Stack for believing in our mission enough to share their life-changing expertise with our team. Their generosity has equipped our nonprofit community theater with a set of principles that have defined our values, developed our leaders, boosted our bottom line, supported our growth, propelled our organization to national attention, and will, hopefully, help ensure our viability for generations to come."

—LORIANNE D. DUNN

"I honestly don't know where we would be without the Great Game and the support of Jack and Betsy Stack. It changed not only the way we do business but the way I run my own finances. It's a no brainer to use the Great Game—it will forever change the way you approach business—I don't know why everyone doesn't play! There's a reason it's called show business."

—BETH DOMANN

"The Great Game of Business embodies such a fundamental philosophical approach that it should be taught in business schools across America. Its concepts of transparency, knowledge, and teamwork empower rather than take advantage of employees to create opportunity and allow them to share in a business's success. From personal experience I can attest that the principles of the Game helped launch our community hospital from distress into a fifteen-year trajectory of growth and success. I believe that Great Game practices represent the greatest opportunity to continue to grow our economy and also to reform our nation's too costly and often irrational healthcare system."

—ALAN KENT

CHANGE THE GAME

CHANGE

SAVING THE AMERICAN DREAM BY CLOSING THE GAP

THE

BETWEEN THE HAVES AND THE HAVE-NOTS

GAME

JACK **STACK**
WITH DARREN DAHL

Advantage®

Published by Advantage, Charleston, South Carolina.
Member of Advantage Media Group.

ADVANTAGE is a registered trademark, and the Advantage colophon is a trademark of Advantage Media Group, Inc.

The Great Game of Business®, Great Game®, A Stake in the Outcome® and The Great Game of Education® are registered trademarks and Critical Number™, MiniGames™, Know & Teach the Rules™, Follow the Action & Keep Score™ are trademarks of The Great Game of Business, Inc. All rights reserved. Registered and/or pending trademarks of The Great Game of Business in the United States and international countries are used throughout this work. Use of the trademark symbols are limited to one or two prominent trademark uses for each mark.

Printed in the United States of America.

10 9 8 7 6 5 4 3 2 1

ISBN: 978-1-64225-129-6
LCCN: 2019909805

Cover design by Jamie Wise.
Layout design by Carly Blake.

This publication is designed to provide accurate and authoritative information in regard to the subject matter covered. It is sold with the understanding that the publisher is not engaged in rendering legal, accounting, or other professional services. If legal advice or other expert assistance is required, the services of a competent professional person should be sought.

Advantage Media Group is proud to be a part of the Tree Neutral® program. Tree Neutral offsets the number of trees consumed in the production and printing of this book by taking proactive steps such as planting trees in direct proportion to the number of trees used to print books. To learn more about Tree Neutral, please visit **www.treeneutral.com**.

TreeNeutral

Advantage Media Group is a publisher of business, self-improvement, and professional development books and online learning. We help entrepreneurs, business leaders, and professionals share their Stories, Passion, and Knowledge to help others Learn & Grow. Do you have a manuscript or book idea that you would like us to consider for publishing? Please visit **advantagefamily.com** or call **1.866.775.1696**.

This book is dedicated to everyone who believes that business can be a powerful force to create positive change in the world. We thank our families, friends, associates, and everyone else we've met along the way who have helped on this journey to develop the Great Game of Business. We'd also like to thank the doubters who didn't think this would work.

CONTENTS

FOREWORD

t is impossible to exaggerate just how isolated and alone Jack Stack and Springfield Remanufacturing Corporation were in 1985 when we first encountered him and learned about the Great Game of Business. By "we," I mean the editorial staff of *Inc.* magazine. Not only had we never heard of any company getting its entire workforce involved in monitoring its financial performance, but the system ran directly contrary to the way every other company in our orbit was managed, including *Inc.* itself. Most private company CEOs we knew considered it dangerous—if not downright insane— to share financial information so broadly inside an organization.

And yet we couldn't help but be intrigued, if only because, on the surface at least, there was a certain logic to the idea behind what later became known as open-book management. What is a business, after all, but a group of people working together to create a product or service that somebody else wants to buy? Why wouldn't you want those people to know how well—or how poorly—they were doing and what it would take to succeed?

That said, we did wonder how the Great Game of Business worked in practice. How was the information disseminated and explained to employees? Did they really buy in? What if the company was struggling and the news was bad? Would the system work in any other type of business? And so on.

Over the past thirty-four years, those questions and many more have been definitively answered. In this book, Jack and his coauthor, Darren Dahl, present case after case of people who have successfully applied the logic and methodology of the Great Game, not only to a wide range of businesses but to not-for-profit organizations and even government entities.

Why has it proven effective in such different settings? No doubt mainly because the premise of the Game is correct. Most people who work for a company, nonprofit, or government agency really *are* capable of understanding what it takes for that entity to achieve its goals, and they're eager to do whatever the situation demands. What's more, they *will* do it as long as they have the information and tools they need to contribute meaningfully.

But there's an even larger reason the Game works so well in so many places, and it has to do with what Dr. Ichak Adizes has identified as the two pillars of any healthy culture—namely, mutual trust and respect. There is no clearer way for leaders to demonstrate the trust and respect they have for their employees than by sharing with them information that is normally kept hidden and treated as confidential and proprietary and by teaching them what the information means and how to use it for the benefit of all.

As Jack has said from the very beginning, it's about appealing to their highest level of thinking. In the following pages, you'll see how they have responded time after time.

Bo Burlingham

Author of *Small Giants* and coauthor of *The Great Game of Business*

PROLOGUE

Business can be a step to make a positive difference in the world. It empowers people to pursue their dreams. The Great Game of Business, the leadership system we developed with the help of our associates, is the result of seeking a better way to run a business than what we had learned on the gritty factory floors where we began our careers. The journey we've been on for more than forty years and counting has been driven by our desire to give people the opportunity to build better lives for themselves, their families, and their communities. Our goal has always been to find a way to teach the have-nots how the haves make it. It's about creating and distributing wealth equitably as a way to close those gaps in wealth that plague our society.

We wrote this book for those of you who continue to seek a brighter side of capitalism, one that truly transforms lives for the better. This book is about hope: no matter how grim things look, you can make them better. You don't have to wait for someone to bail you out. You have the ability to attain peace, security, and happiness. That's what we think the American dream is all about.

It's our continuing belief that it will be through building successful organizations that we can change the world for the better. We can give people the tools to bring about positive change in our society. This book is filled with stories that demonstrate the transformative effects that happen when people embrace a system that makes work fun and rewarding for everyone who plays.

In the pages that follow, we've gathered some of our favorite experiences from the past four decades to show you the system in action and the way it teaches people how to succeed in any kind of organization you can imagine. We want to help answer the question, If this thing is so great, why isn't everyone doing it? The answer, we hope you find, is that there is no reason for any organization not to play the game. All of the stories on the following pages are true. But we decided to use only first names as a way to keep the focus on the ideas and the stories rather than the names and places. As you read, you'll meet real heroes—women and men who have transformed lives, theirs and others', thanks to their courage to find a better way to run an organization.

INTRODUCTION
A TRANSFORMATIONAL JOURNEY

'll never forget the night in June 1980, when I turned on the TV to watch the evening news. It haunts me to this day. We were smack in the middle of a nasty recession, and the news was usually grim, especially in the Rust Belt where I lived and worked. Factories were closing left and right; thousands of people were losing their jobs on a daily basis. Unemployment was soaring, along with interest rates that topped 18 percent. The whole theme of the program on this particular evening was that we, as a society, were losing. America was falling behind. Our standard of living was declining. Lloyd Dobbins, the NBC news anchor that night, said: "Unless we solve the problem of productivity, our children will be the first generation in the history of the US to live worse than their parents."

As a father, I found that hard to hear. It was a kick in the gut. I was thirty-one years old and already had two kids, and a third was on the way. I wondered how my generation was responsible for this downturn, and I didn't want to be blamed for it. I had worked for more than a decade for the same company my dad retired from after working there for forty years. He had always preached that if you worked hard, you could earn opportunity and security. You can't start any lower than I did in working hourly in the mail room of a factory. But I worked hard, and I got ahead—until it all seemed to fall apart. It seemed as if the rules of the game had changed. Maybe we were now playing a different game altogether. Executives became idols as downsizing jobs became the new mantra, laying off people at a time they needed those jobs the most. The focus was on confrontational management. Staying with a company used to mean something; loyalty meant something. That was all coming to an end. I didn't like it. It was like watching the Roman Empire taken apart brick by brick. It felt as if we had lost the American dream.

I began to wonder if we could change that direction. Could we, as a society, improve productivity and get people to believe they could make a difference? Could we find a better way to work and tackle our society's biggest problems together? Could we find hope? I became desperate and turned to every guru and expert out there to try and find answers.

We needed to find a way to boost productivity, morale, and spirit. We needed help in getting more done in less time with fewer resources. We needed to make people more conscious of generating profits—where they come from and where they go—while educating them that business doesn't stop at profit as if it were some pot of gold at the end of the rainbow. Profit is the fuel that creates quality of life. It's profits that update your factory or put in the environmentally friendly lights that create a safe place to work or pay your medical bills. We also needed to teach people how to create wealth in a way that would empower them to fulfill their dreams. But we didn't just want to slap on a patch to treat the symptoms. We wanted a permanent cure.

But how do you teach people these things? I've always believed that people hated chasing the latest management fad or idolizing charismatic leaders. We were looking for a solution that didn't rely on a finger-pointing boss or blaming one another. We wanted to look up to something we could believe in, not what an efficiency expert such as Frederick Taylor would force upon us, as if we were trying to jam a square peg into a round hole. We also wanted something that we could stick to for the long haul. I had seen so many flavors-of-the-month come and go, from management by objectives to total quality management and six sigma. People were always chasing the new thing; they wanted answers just as we did. I had a friend who ran a factory and rallied his team to pursue the prestigious Malcolm Baldrige National Quality Award. Winning the award is a big deal, but so is the stringent application process. It's really, really hard to complete. My friend told me this entire team rallied around the goal, and he invested something like $250,000 to put the company in a position to win. But the night before the winners were to be announced, he confided in me that he hoped his company wouldn't win. I was shocked. "Why did you invest all that time and money then?" I asked. His fear, he told me, was that once they won, he wouldn't know what he could get his team to rally around next. Chasing that award had given them a collective goal to shoot for, but it might not be sustainable if they were to win.

We also wanted to find a way that got everyone working together toward the same goals. That was what was in our hearts and minds. I saw firsthand what happened when you got a team working together. In my time working for International Harvester, we found ways to get one department to outrun another. The difference was that you got everyone involved in running. When you could do that, you could conquer anything.

We were also looking for a system that could teach people to identify strengths and weaknesses and participate in solutions. We didn't want our associates working on the assembly line to think that their peers walking around in sport coats and ties somehow had access to secret information or were taking secret measurements of how hard they were working. Our goal was to find a way to tear down the walls that were a legacy from the command-and-control era in our own factory. We wanted to find a *lasting* leadership system.

Our crazy thought was that we could build one ourselves—a system that we could all manage together. Dating back to my days of working in Melrose Park, I had been deeply influenced by the philosophy of the efficiency guru W. Edwards Deming: when something goes wrong in a business, nine times out of ten, someone is held accountable. Deming, who was one of the positive results of that era, saw that as the Achilles' heel of business. He believed that nine times out of ten, it wasn't a people problem at all; it was a system problem. Rather than

> It is an amazingly freeing effect when you shift to managing a system instead of managing people.

blaming an individual for variances or deviations, you should put your time and energy into improving the system. It is an amazingly freeing effect when you shift to managing a system instead of managing people.

We wondered what kind of system could replace the traditional organizational-chart, top-down-driven model. Work can be boring and tedious. We thought if we could get people pumped up to come to work—to actually want to come to work because they wanted to win—it would be an incredible advantage for us. Our goal was also to bury the mind-set that people should just do their job, nothing more, nothing less. We might call these employees the faceless people or the living dead. They don't look healthy or act in a healthy way. They show up to work just as a means to move on to something else. We wanted to find a way for those jobs to take on more meaning, to help those employees to dream. We wanted to open their eyes to the kind of progress they could make each and every day toward fulfilling their goals—and have fun doing it. We also wanted to make their families proud of them and the difference they were making. One way to do that was to treat business as a game. We had learned one universal truth: people like to win. Tying the idea of games, friendly competition, and having fun at work could be a way to do the right thing in finding a work-life balance. That, we believed, could be the secret to creating a sustainable business, something that could last one hundred years or more.

The result of that experiment was a leadership system that was built on the idea of openness and inclusiveness. It was also about finding a way to have fun at work. When Bo Burlingham and I wrote a book called *The Great Game of Business* about this system we had built in our garage shop in the middle of Missouri, we were clueless about the kind of impact it would have on people. We had absolutely no sense that people would want to come visit us and see if what they had read about us was true or not. The idea that people from other countries would fly into our midwestern city was even more mind boggling. And they came from all over, from Europe and all the way from Asia and Australia. There was even a demand for the book Bo and I wrote to be translated into different languages. Someone even smuggled a copy into Russia. That just blew us away—and further convinced us that we truly had touched a nerve in people that transcends the kinds of cultural and language barriers that can sometimes keep us apart. Business was a way to bring us together.

What we've learned is that the principles of our Great Game system could work just as well in other countries as they do in the United States. Perhaps even cooler is that the system can connect people throughout an organization even when they work in different locations or speak different languages. When you open up the rules of business to anyone, and provide the information to act on, it becomes a kind of glue that holds everyone together while also empowering them to move forward hand in hand.

THE UNIVERSAL LANGUAGE OF CAPITALISM

When the late Supreme Court Justice Louis Brandeis said, "Sunshine is the best disinfectant," he was onto something. The more open and transparent something is, the healthier it is, especially when it comes to the economy or a company's books. I would argue that a primary cause of the most recent global recession that began in 2008 was the failure to open the books on the mortgage loan industry. If these companies had been using the Great Game system, I believe we would have avoided the entire mess, because everyone up and down the line would have been asking more questions. You need to stop a catastrophe at the bottom; trying to fix things at the top is too tricky. And you can do that by opening the books and educating everyone to read them. But because the books remain closed, the same things are still happening today. The investment community continues to make bets with people's money. Yet people don't recognize this as gambling. Without the discipline and openness of the system, we're at risk for even bigger collapses and scandals in the future. Of course, this wasn't the first time that lack of transparency helped wreck not only an industry but the economy of an entire nation.

We saw this firsthand when we were honored to be invited to a nation in Africa, which was, at the time, the jewel of the copper-mining industry. In fact, it was the only job-creating industry the country had. Copper exports represented about 85 percent of the country's gross domestic product (GDP) at the time, and the industry employed between fifty-five thousand and eighty-five thousand workers, the only people with jobs in a country with nine million people. The country was also run by a socialist government. Those eighty-five thousand workers produced the revenue for the healthcare and welfare of those nine million other people, which makes me laugh when I think that we have overhead problems today, here in the United States.

The country was also rocked by inflation to the point where the value of the currency would change by the hour. As we traveled around the country, we would see people cashing their checks by noon instead of waiting until the end of the day. They feared their checks would have less value as the hours went by because the currency was devaluing that quickly. Every resource imaginable was scarce there. When we wrote on only one side of a paper flipchart, people stared at us, wondering why we weren't using the other side of the paper as well. Even an empty bottle of beer was rinsed out and sent back to the brewery to be refilled.

We had been invited by the government and one of the big mining companies there to see if our system could help the mines—and therefore the country's economy—perform better. In fact, the country was at risk of defaulting on its loans and losing control of its mines if things didn't turn around. It was like going back to the industrial revolution in the 1900s. It was all about volume and mass production: pick, pick, shovel, shovel. A penny difference in the price or cost of the metal affected the GDP by something like $10 million.

The mind-set was that the more copper they mined, the better off the country would be.

But until we arrived, most people were not inspired. They would do their job, nothing more. If you gave them a deadline to do something, such as drill a new mine shaft in a mountain by December 19, they would work like crazy to get it done on time. No one ever thought about what could happen if they finished it earlier. Rather than thinking about all the extra copper they could extract or the money they could save, they simply just did what they were told.

We remember meeting one guy who had a gift for separating the copper ore from the dirt. This was an incredibly labor-intensive operation. This guy was big and strong, and his productivity was off the charts—when he showed up for work. Absenteeism was rampant. So were shortages of mining machine parts. That meant that many of the machines critical to the extraction of the copper lay idle for days at a time. When we talked to this highly productive miner and tried to explain that the mine was losing money anytime he wasn't at work and the machines weren't running, he looked at us and smiled. "How can we lose money when there is still copper in the ground?" he asked.

The global tech industry was booming at that time, so high-quality copper was in high demand. One customer was so desperate to receive his copper first that he was willing to pay for it within ten to fifteen days if the shipments went out within the first five days of the month. That could have been a huge boost to the cash flow of the mining operations—if getting the shipments out had been prioritized. If the copper wasn't shipped on time, that customer would delay payment for forty-five to sixty extra days. Those were the terms of the deal. Due to the price fluctuations in the copper market, every minute counted. That meant a delay of even just a few hours in shipping the ore could cost the mining operation millions of dollars in missed sales and the chance of early payment. In other words, the miners had every incentive to get the copper mined, processed, loaded, and shipped as quickly as they could. It was a big logistical puzzle to solve, step by step by step. But as we toured the shipping docks, we learned that a ship had already been loaded but hadn't left yet, even though it was now past the fifth day of the month. We asked the harbor master what was causing the delay. He replied that there wasn't any rush. "What difference would one day make?" he asked. It was a total breakdown in communications. No one had explained to the harbor master the game that was really being played, or what was at stake.

We were there to teach people such as the harbor master and the miners to think as the owners did, to teach them to make money and take control of their mines. If they could improve their cash flow, they could begin to pay down their debt. And once we opened things up, the people were brilliant. Our first meeting was in a stadium in front of about one thousand miners. For about two years, off and on, we worked at it with them. We taught them to play the Great Game system using soccer analogies related to knowing the rules, keeping score, and sharing a stake in the outcome. We built a fifty-five-foot-tall financial statement that showed updated reports on how many tons of copper were produced, the cost per ton, and where the workers stood, relative to the new bonus program we helped them create, which rewarded them for mining the copper more quickly and getting it shipped out on time. We taught them about the rules of the game they were playing and how they could win. We were trying to stimulate their education. We began to help them develop a sense of clarity—and things began to change. We got their efficiency way up; we were getting there. We even began to dream up ideas about how the economy could diversify away from having all its eggs in one copper basket.

The problem was that no one was watching the money guys at the top. Nothing they did was transparent. They were keeping demand, and prices, artificially high by putting in bids after they knew the cost. It was all rigged. After the scandal over price-fixing became public, and the inner workings of the market were brought to light, the price of copper plummeted, and everything just collapsed as a house of cards does. There were many victims, including several global banking conglomerates. Of course, the entire nation suffered too. The mines went bankrupt, the government defaulted on its loans, and the mines were eventually bought by other private companies from around the world, all because the markets lacked the transparency that these people had worked so hard to embrace.

Fortunately, there is a silver lining to this story. While many of the mining jobs disappeared, a lot of the people who were laid off started their own companies, because we taught them the rules of business. We still get pictures and emails from them. One of our favorites was a guy named Banne, who started his own electric motor rewinding company. He even attached a photo of himself smiling in front of some of his equipment. Since we had taught them how business works, folks like Banne had the confidence to start their own business after they lost their job. This is the power of the system. It not only teaches people to think as owners do but it gives them the opportunity to be one. That's how they can help to take steps to ensure that their children might have better lives than they do. They don't have to wait for someone to help them; they can take steps to help themselves. That's the brighter side of capitalism at work.

HISTORY REPEATING ITSELF

The irony is that the thorny issues we faced in the 1980s, and the challenges that African nation dealt with, are no different from what we are facing, as a global society, today. All you need to do is turn on the cable news networks to hear pundits telling us how bad things are and that today's young people around the world are doomed to live a worse life than their parents do. At times, I've felt like Rip Van Winkle waking up after a long sleep.

Everyone knows what the problems are, but nobody is doing anything about it. Everyone's waiting for someone else to come out with the solution, not realizing that each individual has the power to create change without outside help. For all of the doom and gloom, we still have a chance to turn things around. For more than forty years, we have been crafting a leadership system built on common sense that truly brings people together and empowers them to chase their own dreams no matter how much the odds seem stacked against them. All you need is the desire to start playing something we call the you-gotta-wanna. When you have that, you can begin to change the world, one transformation at a time.

CHAPTER ONE
A LASTING MANAGEMENT SYSTEM

You can't imagine how much grief my associates and I have received over the forty years or so since we began calling our business leadership system the Great Game of Business. I've lost count of how many times people have told us something along the lines of business being a serious occupation, not a game.

Maybe if we had a mulligan on that, a do-over, we'd call it something else. But it's important to remember that we weren't doing this for anyone else; this was just for us. We weren't thinking about how to brand something for public use. We never dreamed it would take on a life of its own. It was just our nutty notion that we thought we could teach anyone to be a businessperson just as we could teach anyone to play a board or video game decades before anyone dreamed up the term *gamification,* whatever that is. A single common thread that runs through us all is the desire to win. We wanted to create an accelerated learning process that would register with people. We knew that games can engage people in learning and that the biggest doubter can crack with the help of a game.

We started with the premise that there are three keys to successfully playing a game—the fundamentals:

1. **You need to know the rules.**

2. **You need to follow the action and keep score.**

3. **You need to provide a stake in the outcome, a reward for when you win.**

We saw those three elements as critical to moving our business forward, not unlike how an engine, a transmission, and a set of wheels power a car along the highway. You need all three things to work in alignment if you want to get anywhere.

1. KNOW AND TEACH THE RULES

The premise of starting to play our Game is not unlike learning to play a card game such as gin, something I have been teaching my grandkids. The idea is to just start playing. Then you teach the other players the rules as you go. Some people pick up the rules really quickly, while others might take longer. They might even get frustrated at times. But that's where the dedication to practicing will eventually pay off: the players begin to think about more than just playing; they want to win. They also begin to see that there is a strategy to winning.

Most people don't think there are any rules in business. They don't realize there is really a structure to it. Maybe a lot of them just haven't read the directions and have made up their own conclusions instead. It's as if they've been given a jigsaw puzzle without the picture on the box. How can you put the pieces together if you don't know what you're trying to build?

There is something ironic about the fact that we have had generations of accountants who have created a system built on entry after entry and regulation after regulation, all to help create a sense of safety in the numbers of a business. And yet there are still many people who don't trust businesses or their numbers. They think there's always another set of books or some trick being played on them. People have told me that business is nothing but cronyism, that the only way to succeed is to be born with a silver spoon in your mouth.

I read an article about a mathematics professor who found that most kids don't like math because they think there is a trick behind it. They don't trust it. Here we have a very logical system that everyone in the world has been using for more than five hundred years, and yet many people don't trust it. Back in 1494, Luca Pacioli, the Franciscan friar and mathematician who popularized double-entry accounting, wrote, "A person should not go to sleep at night until the debits equal the credits." Brother Luca would be turning over in his grave if he knew how many people ignore his advice these days. People don't know the fundamental rules of business or, at least, have an open enough mind to learn them. That's the gap between the haves and the have-nots. When you close your mind to new things, you become resistant to change. Is it really a surprise, then, that people get into debt and run into financial problems all because they refuse to educate themselves about something as simple as a compounded fraction?

We weren't interested in teaching anyone accounting, which I have found is a subject most people fear as much as they do public speaking. What we wanted to teach is probably more accurately called business literacy or maybe even common sense business. We wanted everyone in the business to understand how the money that comes in as sales revenue eventually finds its way to the bottom line in the form

15

of profit—or loss. We wanted people to track the numbers to ensure we got off on the right foot, didn't go backward, and didn't outrun our coverage. Our whole idea was to build a system of continuous improvement for the organization. We believed you can't be successful unless you use numbers in a disciplined way.

The whole intent in teaching the rules of business is to help people in the organization get a better sense of the big picture, of where the organization is going so they can then decide if it's a place they can prosper in. Is it worth investing their time there? The numbers, some more than others, help people get at the truth.

At the same time, people who start their own businesses and overlook the rules start off on the wrong foot, which sets off a whole series of repercussions.

For example, a trap many entrepreneurs fall into if they don't know the rules is not looking far enough ahead. They're not planning two, five, or ten years into the future. There is real power in forward thinking and giving people what they need to know to make the vision a reality. What we've done at our company, for example, is incredible. The severe recession of 2009 hit us hard. So we got everyone in the company involved in setting our strategic goals through our High Involvement Planning (HIP) process. We set out on a ten-year journey to save $100 million to protect ourselves from the next economic downturn and potential loss of jobs. Just by putting that audacious goal out there and focusing on it every year, we're 97 percent toward our goal. We'll likely reach it a year early, in fact. That wasn't an accident; that was a plan. Strategic thinking is about minimizing risks and maximizing rewards. It's about looking at the forest instead of the trees. You need to have the courage to make hard moves even during the best of times. And you do that by addressing your weaknesses.

Maybe that's difficult for start-ups and young entrepreneurs to understand. Maybe it's easier for older companies, such as ours, that have been around for decades. I think that, maybe, the younger companies need an opportunity to learn from the ones that have been around for a while. But it's almost as if they believe they have a new set of rules to run their companies by.

It's worth remembering that entrepreneurs from the 1980s, when we started our business, were thrown out onto the streets when the big companies started laying everyone off. But we had learned some things about the parameters of business before they kicked us aside. Today, kids are taught to raise money with nothing more than an idea and no experience whatsoever in building a business. Their teachers fail to explain the emotional strings that come attached to borrowing money. I think there is a big gap here. These students are not made aware of the misery and the pain they'll go through in raising money, or how they will have sleepless nights worrying about making the payroll, or letting down the people who lent them the money. It can be a horrific experience if they don't know the rules. But when people are taught the basics, the real magic begins.

People are often surprised that the Game is far more than just about sharing the financials. People think the Game is just about money, when it's really about building quality of life. It's about promoting teamwork and engagement at levels you might not think were possible. It's about connecting the dots between what you do as an individual and how you affect the goals you and your coworkers share. The Game is really all about the psychological side of work, not just about doing a job. It's about turning something that could be boring or menial and making it fun and participatory. It's not about watching and heckling from the sidelines. It's about everyone being engaged in the action and helping the team win. What we learned over time is that the more knowledge you share with your people, the more freeing and fun your job becomes.

Some of these lessons came from the days when my dad coached me in baseball. My dad was a local legend in Chicago, a left-handed outfielder who could fly. He might have had a big-league future if he hadn't volunteered to serve in WWII or had a growing family to support. After the war, he was invited to participate in spring training. But he got appendicitis and was laid up for eight weeks, recovering from the operation. He missed his chance. After he recovered, he started playing softball on the weekends, which is when he learned he could make some real money. He would start on a Sunday with $10 and come home with $100. He was good, really good. I don't remember him ever having to buy a beer when we went to bars where they knew him from his playing days.

As my coach, my dad would drill the idea into me that playing baseball was 75 percent a psychological exercise and only 25 percent a physical exercise. He wanted me to think ahead about how to play the game. He would lose his temper when he saw me hit the ball where an infielder or outfielder was standing. "You have to look up and hit the ball into the holes!" he would holler at me. "Hit 'em where they ain't!" I would often just roll my eyes, thinking, *Really, Dad?*

While that point seemed obvious, executing it was something else. I knew the basics by then: how to swing the bat, how to catch the ball, and how to run the bases. But it seemed as if my dad would always find the one thing I missed and grill me on it. What he was trying to teach me was the strategy behind the game. He wanted me to see the power in thinking ahead and creating a plan before I went to bat or took the field. He wanted me to identify the weaknesses and opportunities that the other team was giving my teammates and me so we could take advantage of them.

It's like the story of the Oakland A's in Michael Lewis's book

Moneyball. As a team that could never compete with their rivals in budgetary terms, they needed to innovate. They needed to find new opportunities their opponents had overlooked and leverage every dollar they had. That's how they found inefficiencies in the market. While other teams paid top dollar for sexy home-run hitters, the A's saw the value in players who knew how to take a walk and get on base. Other teams laughed at the Oakland A's players, some of whom didn't have the look of a major leaguer—until those other teams started losing games to the Oakland A's. Then, every team started looking for that same kind of player and those same kinds of pattern.

What about how teams such as the Tampa Bay Rays innovated by using the shift—infielders move around the diamond based on where a particular player is likely to hit the ball—as a way to get into the heads of batters? Even though they might leave an entire side of the infield open, many hitters refused to—or simply couldn't—adjust, even after they hit out after out.

The point is that teams such as the A's and the Rays put their individual egos and skill sets aside in an effort to try something new to win games as a team. Knowing the rules knocks down the walls and puts everyone on a level playing field. You become part of something bigger than yourself.

I applied those same lessons when I coached my kids in Little League. Our mantra was to teach our kids situational baseball and winning as a team. Rather than focus on individual drills as every other team did, we worked on situational skills. We would run through imaginary scenarios. We would make sure every player knew the rules and how to use them to gain an edge. It was a lot more fun than running drills. Plus, it kept everyone focused on the real goal, which was to win as a team.

In one play we practiced, when the other team had a runner on base, our right fielder would creep up behind the first base bag. Then our pitcher would throw over to first but pretend to overthrow the first baseman, making it look like an error. The runner on base would then take off for a second, not realizing that the throw had actually gone to our sneaky right fielder, who just happened to have a rocket arm. He would then throw a laser beam to second base to nab the runner. When it was flawlessly executed, it was a thing of beauty to watch.

Some of the other parents found these methods too unconventional. Fathers, sometimes from both teams, would come down from the stands, yelling at us to play baseball the traditional way.

A lot of people think about business that way: they are not taught to think differently or to look up and see the opportunities in front of them. Our goal, both in coaching baseball, and in coaching businesspeople, is to work on the psychological side of the game.

I'll never forget this one game we played: we faced a pitcher who was out of a nightmare movie, a huge kid who seemed to be a foot taller than anyone else on the field—and he threw fireballs. Even when he was just warming up—*whap!*—the sound of that ball hitting the catcher's glove was like a thunder clap.

I remember when my son, who batted lead-off for the team, stood in to bat when he saw the pitcher shake off the catcher, meaning he wanted to throw a different pitch. My son called time out and looked back into the dugout. His eyes widened, and he shook his head as if to say, "He has more than one pitch? What am I supposed to do now?"

He was right. We were in real trouble. This hulk on the mound was striking everyone out. Our kids couldn't do anything. The good news was that our pitcher and fielders were playing a flawless game as well. All we needed to do was to find a way to score a run or two. After the end of one inning, when the kids came back into the dugout to take their next turn at bat, I put the challenge to them: What could we do differently to get some runners on base?

That was when one of our players pointed out that the other team's pitcher was throwing so hard and his curveballs moved so much that the catcher couldn't hold the ball most of the time. Our guy suggested that if our players swung and missed on a third strike, and the catcher dropped the ball, our hitter could run to first base. And if they could beat the throw from the catcher, they'd be awarded the base.

This was a great idea, especially since speed was one of our strengths. Our kids, many of them soccer players as well, were fast. If they could get on base, they could also put pressure on the other team by stealing second—and then third—whenever they got the chance.

Another player observed that when one of our players squared to bunt, the pitcher got wild. He also noticed that the pitcher, while intimidatingly tall, wasn't very agile when it came to fielding his position. If the hitters could bunt the ball to areas where he had to make a play, it might take him out of his rhythm.

It was a stroke of genius!

We brought the boys together and explained what they needed to do: bunt early in the count whenever possible, and whenever they had two strikes, swing away and hustle down the line to first base. If they got there, they should be aggressive and try to steal the extra base whenever they could. I was so proud that these players, even at the ages of ten and eleven, were willing to think beyond their own individual achievements. They weren't trying to hit the game-winning home run all by themselves. They had found a way to win as a team.

Even as our first batter headed toward home plate to take his turn at bat, you could almost feel the momentum shift. Granted, squaring up to bunt against this kid took guts—and maybe even a silent prayer. As the pitcher reared back and let his fastball rip, the hitter just laid his bat over the plate and let the pitch hit it. *Doink!* The ball dribbled out toward the mound, where the pitcher awkwardly tried to reach down and pick it up. When he did, he unleashed his cannon to try and beat the runner—and promptly sailed his throw over his first baseman's mitt. We had a base runner!

After that, it was pandemonium as we kept repeating that pattern: bunt or swing through the third strike and bust a gut running to get to first to beat the throw. Then the runners would take big leads and tear off toward second or third whenever they got the chance. You could see the pitcher visibly getting red in the face with frustration. Soon enough, we had loaded the bases and hadn't even gotten a hit.

Now the pitcher was really rattled. He kept peeking over his shoulder at the runner on third, wondering what we might be up to next. Then, just as the pitcher began his windup, our runner on third took off, sprinting toward home. It was a race! After the dust settled around the plate, the umpire called out, "Safe!" Our runner had stolen home, and we had our first run.

This prompted the opposing coach to share some choice words with me. Whoa! Just as those parents had, he complained that we weren't playing the game the traditional way. I couldn't have cared less. Our team had found a weakness in the opposition, and they were going to exploit it in every way they could. That came from teaching them to think beyond the individual fundamentals to all winning together.

In the end, we won that game, one to nothing, and none of our players ever got a hit.

What's interesting is that many of the kids from that team ended up being really good strategic thinkers and really successful in their lives and careers. Can we tie that back to playing on that team? Maybe not entirely, but I think some of those lessons stuck, especially what they learned about looking beyond themselves, as individuals, to being members of a team—and a community.

To be successful in life, you have to be going somewhere. That's especially true in the business world. And you need to get everyone on your team involved in getting you there. While that might seem obvious, it's something a lot of people miss. You'll always have a better chance of winning if everyone on the team knows what it takes to win.

2. KEEP SCORE

As a grandfather to ten beautiful grandchildren, I spend a lot of weekends in gyms or out on the soccer fields, watching these kids tear around. I think that's why a scene from the movie *Parental Guidance*, starring Billy Crystal and Bette Midler, continues to stick with me. Billy, who plays a professional baseball announcer, is sitting in the stands, watching his grandson pitch for his Little League team. The grandson rears back and throws a pitch, and the hitter swings and misses. Billy is ecstatic as he calls out, "Strike one!" Then, as the hitter swings through the second pitch, Billy yells out, "Strike two!" Now he's really excited as the third pitch comes in, and as the batter misses again, Billy stands up and calls, "Strike three! Yer outa there!" But nobody else seems to notice as the pitcher, catcher, and umpire all get back into position. That's when Billy calls out to the umpire, "Hey, Blue, three strikes! He's out!" The umpire walks over to Billy and explains calmly that they don't count outs in this game; the kids keep hitting until they get on base. "Seriously?" Billy asks. The umpire just nods his head, almost in embarrassment. "Then how do you know who's winning?" Billy asks. "We don't keep score," the umpire says. "Every game ends in a tie."

Apparently lots of sports are played by kids who don't keep score. I don't understand this. There's nothing wrong with getting beat. We need to be teaching our kids to handle defeat because that's what happens in the real world. And you can't do that if you're not keeping score.

The whole idea of the scorecard is to create some excitement, some adrenaline, to give people something to get pumped up about. We don't get excited enough at work, in my opinion. We don't find those opportunities to have more fun. When you have access to the information and the data, you can't help but get excited to come to work to see if you can do better than you did the day before. It's about achievement. And once you establish a pattern of winning, you truly begin to feel good about yourself. This isn't a lesson we are teaching our young people.

Keeping score helps validate the rules of the Game: When you take action, you can see the results on the scoreboard in terms of the numbers and the financials. You can see how you make a difference, and you can go home at night feeling good about yourself. Keeping score gives you something important to talk about, and communication is something you need to live and breathe every day in your organization. It's your daily vitamins.

The catch is that most organizations track too many numbers and KPIs, which people find too complicated and confusing. That's what I love about our system, which starts with the critical number, the one thing that can sink a company. Knowing your critical number is having the courage to face your worst nightmare, the thing that could hurt you the most, and doing something about it before it comes true. And that's something that changes every year, based on how your biggest weakness evolves. Having that on your scorecard gets you focused on coming up with incredible ways to improve it, ways you might not have believed you could have come up with otherwise. Those improvements are the result of attention to detail. The art of planning begins with the assumption that something will go wrong.

A lot of people get caught by unexpected surprises because they don't keep score of where they stand at all times. You need to know where the shoe will drop and how you can catch it before it hits the ground.

In our company, for instance, one recent critical number was our employee retention rate, which we needed to increase from 73 percent to 90 percent. We did this because everyone at that time was facing a massive shortage of workers. By setting that goal and keeping score, all these wonderful things began to happen to drive us toward that number. And as that number began to improve, people's lives improved because they could work less overtime and therefore enjoy more time with their families. When you choose and track the right critical number, it has a massive domino effect on six to ten things in the organization. That's how you can generate incredible productivity.

Once people know the rules of the game they are in, and they learn how to keep score, they begin to look for more sophisticated ways to win, to innovate. They also begin to realize how they can work together, no matter what industry they are in or what cultural barriers might exist, because they are using the scoreboard as part of the system.

3. SHARE A STAKE IN THE OUTCOME

We start by teaching people the rules of the marketplace. Then we show them how to keep score. Once they have those legs of the stool in place, they better understand how they can win and earn their share of a stake in the outcome. It's motivational. It gives people a strong voice in daily decision making and in planning the kind of future they want. And in the case of a company where there is broad-based ownership, it can also give people a chance to create a lot of wealth based on their shared success. When you're an owner, you're not thinking just about the day-to-day; you're thinking about the future.

Over the years, though, we have found that companies that might be attracted to the Game get nervous when it comes to sharing ownership. We've heard all kinds of reasons why it won't work for them. Many people believe in the fallacy that transferring ownership means giving something away, that employees don't deserve to share in the success of the firm. We obviously don't think this way. A company is only as good as its people. Our belief is that unless you bring in people as real owners, you are setting limits to how far they can go. The more you educate people, the more they want to know. And the more your people are taught to think and act as owners do, the better the decisions they make to create a bigger pie that everyone can benefit from.

To get those better decisions, you sometimes have to give your people the information and let them come up with a solution. That's also how you give someone a stake in the outcome.

Consider a story that I heard from Tim, a general manager at one of our factories. During the weekly huddles and monthly planning meetings, many of our frontline hourly people began to voice complaints about their wages. They wanted raises. Even the extra money they were earning through their variable compensation gain share program wasn't enough.

Our business has seen the shares of our employee stock ownership program (ESOP), skyrocket in recent years. But the wealth our people were earning for the long term wasn't helping them pay for the bills they faced from day to day. Sometimes short-term needs demand attention at the very time when you don't have the cash to pay for anything, even, say, for day care or the mortgage.

At the same time, our people were constantly hearing stories from their friends and family members that other companies were paying higher wages to try to bring in new employees. Our people began to ask why we weren't matching those pay hikes. Some people even left their job with us just to get an extra $1 an hour. We were facing a weakness.

To put this all in context, this factory competes in a highly commoditized market where every penny makes a difference in whether a product line is profitable or not. Our biggest expense, of course, is the cost of labor. About two-thirds of our people are paid on an hourly basis. Part of our education program focuses on explaining how pay hikes affect the bottom line and how, by remaining profitable, we increase the value of the business, which everyone benefits from through their shares in the ESOP. If we could, we would pay everyone $50 an hour. But the math simply doesn't work if you want to sustain the company over a long period of time.

The disconnect between long-term wealth building and short-term wage gaps was a problem, and it needed to be dealt with. But rather than coming up with a top-down solution, Tim let people come up with their own answer. He recruited a group of ten volunteers who had recently completed a round of financial literacy training. It was a diverse group of men and women who represented just about every functional area of the factory, from assemblers to warehouse workers. The team represented a diverse cross-section of our community as well. Tim told me the group members had really bonded during their training, even going so far as to give themselves a team name—the Determinators—because they were so determined to understand every nuance of the income statement. They were now ready for a new and tougher challenge.

As a kickoff, Tim, along with the controller and HR manager, bought the team lunch and laid out the problem with the wage gap. The team was told they could have access to any company information they wanted, and they were also encouraged to seek anything they needed from outside as well. Their challenge was to come up with a solution that was both wage competitive with the market and would also deliver a safe return to the company.

For the next eight weeks, the Determinators dug into the factory's income statement, balance sheet, and cash-flow statement to see how a pay raise would affect the business. These folks really went after it: they bounced ideas off each other, they polled our sister companies for their wage levels, and they even began to look for other ways the factory could reduce costs so they could apply the savings to the payroll.

It's important to point out that this skunk works team could have proposed a $50-an-hour raise. The general manager never put any limits on them. He trusted them to understand the impact of whatever decision they arrived at. It was up to them to debate the impact on the value of the business of whatever course of action they recommended.

After the first five weeks, the team presented their initial plan: They suggested an across-the-board raise of $1 an hour for the one hundred hourly workers. Tim then went to a whiteboard that had the factory's income statement printed on it and flowed through what a $1-an-hour increase looked like. It was a sizable investment for that number of people. Tim simply asked the team to look at the results and asked if they were satisfied with the risk that such a raise involved. "Do you guys think this kind of investment will generate a return for the business?" he asked. "And do you think it will keep us competitive and allow us to make the gain-share program?" They shook their heads no. They wanted to dig deeper and see if they could find a better answer. Specifically, they wanted to get better data on the cost of turnover to quantify how the raise might pay for itself.

Eventually, after a lot of number crunching based on several different scenarios, the group came up with a revised proposal to raise hourly wages by fifty cents across the board for the first six months of the year, followed by another fifty-cent raise six months later if the factory hit its targets. The team's rationale was that the added cost to the payroll would be offset by significantly reducing turnover and the cost of replacing workers on the line. As a way to further reduce the risk and to help ensure the second-half raise could go into effect, Tim and the team put together a short-term incentive plan, which we call a MiniGame, based on overhead variances in the business.

It was a great plan on paper, but the whole company would need to achieve their goals to make everything happen. This was a plan nobody could complain about, but if people wanted to, they could talk to the team who put the plan together rather than blame management. For Tim, that was an investment worth its weight in gold. "Any time we ever put in a raise in the past, we could never please everybody," Tim told me. "Someone always felt slighted. This time was different. It wasn't management who had come up with it; it was the people on the front lines who brought it to their peers." Even better, the time and energy those ten associates invested in the project elevated to an entirely new level their ability to think and act as owners do.

This is just such a great example of what happens when you trust your people enough to give them a stake in the outcome and empower them to do something about it. They had a say in the solution and they made a difference. The Game really gets cooking when people begin to look further out to develop longer-term strategies to win. They also learn how they personally stand to gain from those wins, and how that becomes a ripple effect that spills into their personal lives and communities. When that happens, everyone wins.

CHAPTER TWO
CULTURAL TRANSFORMATION

I n the spring of 2007, a sobering scene began to play out on my TV and the TVs of millions of other Americans across the country. News reports announced that the world was coming to an end. People were confused and fear began to spread everywhere. The housing market was collapsing. So, too, was the banking industry, especially on Wall Street. A lot of people began to wonder how bad things might get. Some even speculated on whether things might get as bad as they had been during the Great Depression that began in the 1930s. No one knew much, which was what made things worse.

Most business owners hate uncertainty, and when things start to look bad, many of them begin to make moves to protect themselves and their stakeholders. In other words, they begin to cut jobs or shut the doors altogether. Back then, if you had a business that was only marginally profitable, and you were afraid demand might dry up, you felt you had no option but to shut down. Businesses of all kinds—banks, retail shops, construction companies—were closing at a disturbing rate.

That's why if you turned on your TV in 2009, you were likely to hear a news story or two about a local business that was laying people off or, worse, closing up shop altogether.

That's what happened in one city in Kentucky. One March day, all the news channels carried the same story: the manufacturing subsidiary of a big multinational company would be closing its doors by the end of the year, taking more than eighty jobs with it. And those job losses were happening at the very time when alternative jobs were hard to find.

One of the plant's leaders was a guy named Rob, who also happened to be a West Point graduate and former soldier. The news came as a shock to Rob and his team. "It was tough for everyone," he later told me. "They were mad, sad, outraged, both at the company and at me."

Adam, another manager at the plant, said he had worked at the plant long enough to know everyone. "You knew who had just bought a new house, or a truck, or who had a baby on the way," he told me. "And then they all just found out they were going to lose their job."

Maybe it was because they had their backs up against the wall or maybe it was because they just couldn't give up, but Rob, Adam, and a few of their colleagues weren't ready to accept that their plant—which made, on an enormous scale, high-tech mining equipment such as drive shafts that weighed more than ten thousand pounds—was going to disappear. So they threw a Hail Mary pass: they contacted us and our management team and asked if we would be interested in buying their operation.

After taking a look at the plant and its people, who were highly skilled at what they did and just as passionate about doing it, I was struck by the similarity of their situation to our experience in our business, Springfield Remanufacturing Corporation (SRC), in 1982. This was a group of people who had never been taught how they could have a positive impact on their business. And now it was too late—unless we offered them a lifeline. But we also had to understand whether the company would be a fit for us.

Since the start of our business, we have acquired or invested in more than sixty different ventures. We think of these expansions as ways to fuel not only our company's growth, but also the careers of our associates. Practicing our system helps us cultivate leaders throughout the organization, and we like to create opportunities for those leaders either by acquiring companies or investing in companies that our associates start. Because

> **Practicing our system helps us cultivate leaders throughout the organization.**

we have been successful with acquisitions and joint ventures, we see a lot of opportunities like the one that this factory was offering.

The one big question we had—the elephant in the room—was whether the team was capable of transforming their culture. These experienced workers had not only become fairly set in their ways but had been trained in an extremely top-down, hierarchical system, a command-and-control environment typical of quality-focused companies such as Toyota. No one did anything until told to. These guys could build a heck of a product; they just didn't know how to build a company because no one had ever taught them how to. Could they really adopt our Great Game system and learn to work from the bottom up? Could they learn to think and act as owners do?

Long story short, we made the deal. To protect our end of the investment, though, we had to turn the operation around and make it cash flow positive within thirty-six months or we would run out of money. The next step was to convince the eighty employees, whose average age was in the midfifties, that they could turn things around by embracing our system.

After the acquisition, I arranged to give a speech in the factory. I planned to tell the team about the challenge and the opportunity ahead of them. To prepare them, we sent over a bunch of copies of *The Great Game of Business*. But I knew it would be a tough sell.

The more I thought about what I was going to say to them, the more I realized I had given almost the exact same speech to the factory workers in Springfield in 1983. When I told them we would be successful only by opening our books, they looked at me as if I had just fallen out of a tree.

The first question they asked me was, "How old are you anyway?" (I was thirty-three, for what it's worth.) You see, Missouri is the show-me state, and these guys didn't want promises; they wanted action.

"Sure, you'll open the books," they said. "Show me."

"Sure, we'll get to make our own decisions. Show me."

Well, we showed those folks in Springfield by creating jobs, distributing wealth, and making our community better. When I visited this factory, I felt I was going back in time to convince one hundred people coming from a very different corporate culture that the system could work for them too. I knew I had my work cut out for me.

A NEW BEGINNING

As I stood before all those people on the factory floor and started talking about SRC and the Great Game and what it means, I immediately saw a difference from what I had seen back in 1982. Where in

Springfield there had been stubbornness, here at this factory I saw a willingness to give the system a try. These folks were used to working for a big, stable company that they were all loyal to. They had already been through the valley of death thinking their factory was going to be shut down. Now, we were here to give them another chance, and they were more than willing to roll the dice.

I told them we wanted to learn from their skills in making high-tech mining equipment. In return, we would teach them the financial skills that were necessary to maintain a sustainable and profitable operation, and, I explained, after one year, they would be eligible to join our ESOP. I said we had thirty-six months to build something great, to leave a legacy. I also told them that ownership meant nothing if they didn't have a voice. We would teach them to speak that language, which would help them take their operation to another level.

I explained that I believed in decentralization and the wisdom of crowds, and that ownership began from the bottom up, not the top down. "We'll help you," I told them. "But it's up to you guys to set the forecasts and the work plans. You will be the ones responsible for the success of this operation. When I leave here today, it will be up to you to make it work. You will set your own standards."

As I continued talking, a different expression began to spread across the faces in front of me. I began to see fear, maybe even terror. I was telling them we were cutting the umbilical cord, which was a terrifying message for these people. As I wrapped up and asked if anyone had questions, only two hands went up, both from women, even though the work force was 90 percent male.

The first woman asked, "How does this motivate us?"

The second asked, "How can we diversify to bring in business from outside mining?" They were both great questions, the answers to which, I told them, they would have to figure out on their own.

Afterward, the factory put on a celebratory picnic lunch for us. And as I talked with Rob, I sensed he was beginning to grasp the magnitude of what employee ownership and open-book management could do. This guy had fought tooth and nail to keep the factory open and save the jobs. He realized he had to produce, and he had the factory humming on the track of continuous improvement and lean manufacturing. Now, we needed to take the employees into entrepreneurial mode.

Something interesting happened over lunch. The employees had put together a great spread of hamburgers, hot dogs, chips, potato salad—the works. They had a cake big enough to feed an army. As we sat around tables covered with red-and-white-checkered tablecloths, I chewed the fat with some of the guys about all the great products they had worked on over the years: the tractors they'd built, the dump trucks they'd rehabbed. They had made or fixed some of the biggest and toughest machines around. As if to make that point, sitting right next to one of the tables was a huge pivot shaft that fit into the transmission of one the tractors they had manufactured. It was an impressive piece of machinery.

As we continued to chat, I mentioned that the lunch spread was impressive, which prompted a young man at the end of the table to say that he and his wife had put it together themselves. Without prompting, this guy, JJ, began rattling off how much he'd spent on the meat, the buns, even the propane he used for cooking. To save money, his wife had baked that huge cake, which was chocolate on one side and vanilla on the other. The total cost of the cake's ingredients was $45. I could tell JJ was proud that even though he was given a budget of $500, he had spent only $463, and he knew down to the dollar where it had all gone. Meanwhile, sitting next to the cake was that giant pivot shaft. No one in the room had any idea how much it had cost to build the shaft.

The next day, I called JJ to thank him. I told him that what he had done with that picnic was a perfect example of how the Great Game works. "If everyone starts thinking as you do," I told JJ, "your factory will be outrageously successful."

When I have shared the mining factory story with people, I haven't always gotten a positive response, particularly the part where I tell the people from the shop floor that it is up to them to figure out how to make things work. People have said to me, "You can't just abandon your employees."

This attitude misses the point. We weren't letting people fend for themselves; we were empowering them to make decisions for themselves. There is a huge difference.

From day one, we began teaching our system to the people at the mining equipment factory as a way for them to transform their business. Rather than being told by me or a manager how they needed to transform it, they got to make those choices themselves.

Our goal was to turn the pyramid upside down. We couldn't lift the employees up. They needed to do that for themselves. That's why the first thing I told them was that I was there to learn from them. But that didn't mean they didn't have our support. We're from the show-me state, so of course we were showing them how to play the game. But they still had to play for themselves.

Through our system, they learned strategy, relationship building, talent development and, above all, adapting to change. We were teaching them a system in which each and every associate understands how to make a difference in the financial performance of their company.

The key to this company's surviving and thriving lay in its people's need to feel invested and start acting as if they were owners. That's how you win at playing the Game. But no one can make someone have that feeling; it comes from within. All we can do is put it out there. It's up to each individual to reach out and grab the brass ring. It's up to all individuals to decide whether to play, to decide if they have the you-gotta-wanna or not.

AN ANNUAL CHECK-UP

About a year after the acquisition, I visited the mining equipment factory to see for myself if things were changing or not. Rob told me the biggest change for him and the other associates at the factory was having access to the financial information they needed to understand what was going on—the good and the bad—and how they could do their jobs better. "Open book doesn't always paint a rosy picture," Rob said. "But everyone can now see how their suggestions and contributions can improve things, which is very motivating."

As Rob and I walked the shop floor, he told me story after story of how people in the plant—not the management team—were making the biggest difference. Because managing the cost of parts and materials is so central to the success of a remanufacturing business, the associates were completely rethinking how they went about their jobs on a daily basis. They kept coming up with new ways to save and reuse materials, savings that went right to their bottom line.

A machinist, Tony, after learning how much it cost to outsource the machining of engine blocks, found a way to do it himself. Rick, another machinist, figured out a way to convert scrap material from old engine cylinder liners to make sleeves used in repairing transmission parts rather than buying new sleeves.

In fact, the associates figured out so many ways to avoid using new parts that they created a whole new problem: They were buying and returning too many new parts, which was becoming a big hassle for the planners and parts-handling team. Through the efforts of assemblers such as Paul, who cut his returns down to two or fewer per job, overall returns were cut by 70 percent in just over three months, reducing costs, increasing efficiency, and improving cash flow.

Rob told me that he and his associates had found other ways to become more productive and flexible. "We used to operate on the idea that an employee was hired to do one thing and one thing only," he told me. "We now know we can't afford that kind of specialization."

For instance, the company used to employ a full-time painter, who painted all the parts that came out of the plant, such as the engines and the transmissions. Then, an employee named Mike stepped up to get the job done in a few hours each day before he moved on to other tasks. Larry, an assembler, learned to build hydraulic motors when someone from the department was needed someplace else. Several machinists learned to run multiple machines at the same time, which was something they had never had the incentive to do before.

"I have to admit there was some skepticism about the Game in the beginning," Rob told me. "Everyone needed some time to dig in and understand how it worked. Now, each of us can see how we can make a difference. The more we learned, the more our morale went up."

Less than a year after they joined the SRC family, sales were already better than expected and the team had met or exceeded its financial targets through the first two quarters of the year. Rob and his team turned their business on its head. Sales were substantially higher than over the same period the year before due to increased demand for powertrains and hydraulic equipment. Rob and his team also came up with ideas for new products such as axles, transmissions, and power modules.

In fact, the associates earned a first-quarter bonus as a result of the progress they'd made in tackling their critical number, which more than doubled their profit projections. The main drivers behind those results were the continual cost improvements engineered by Rob and his associates.

That early success at the mining equipment factory validated our belief that the strength of the company was its people. It was like that puzzle I mentioned earlier: they had the puzzle pieces, and we gave them the picture and let them figure out how to put it all together. They learned to not only build products but also a company.

Of course, Rob and his team knew they still had a lot of work ahead of them, particularly when it came to further diversifying their products and customers. They knew they had all their eggs in one basket. "Before," Rob told me, "people used to just come to work, collect a paycheck, and assume it would always be there. Now, everyone here is really interested in the business and is working toward trying to diversify it because we know what's at stake if we don't."

They took major steps forward when they hired a full-time sales representative and shipped their first new product, a transmission, to a new customer. That was a big moment in terms of diversifying the company's customer base.

But Rob and his team knew there was more work to do in their diversification efforts in areas such as continually reducing their product return rate, streamlining their product-development process, and cutting back on their lead times, all while trying to improve their customer-satisfaction ratings.

As time went on, perspectives on the factory floor changed dramatically. "It was amazing to see the people who built the engines and transmissions become financially literate," Rob told me. "They began to understand fairly well what was going on in the business. As a result, their confidence went up and the business began to transform."

In the beginning, after their parent company had dropped the bomb on them, the associates were simply worried about keeping their jobs. Then, as the company's financial performance improved, that focus began to shift to earning a bonus and wiping out weaknesses. Once they accomplished that, they began to set their sights on an even bigger prize: ownership.

The plan was to enroll the factory associates in an ESOP, over time, which generated a lot of energy and some confusion.

While the associates increasingly used their weekly huddles to educate themselves on the ESOP program, the associates also created what we call an ownership culture committee (OCC), which, in this case, was a team made up of four associates from different levels in the company. The goal of the committee was to serve as an intermediary between the management and the associates on the plant floor while promoting an ownership culture and, ultimately, driving better performance.

As the company began to make the transition to an employee-owned business, the OCC captured some of the mood of the associates.

For example, Jason, an electrician by trade who eventually became a maintenance technician, was from a small town in the mountains and had worked mostly for contractors before joining the company. Working for a company that listened to his ideas and opinions was new to him. "I was used to doing what I was told to get my paycheck," he told the OCC. "What we do now is a whole lot different than that." He was excited about the changes, especially the idea of becoming an owner. "I think the idea of employee ownership is the biggest motivator there is," Jason said. "I think it's exciting because I can personally impact the price of the stock we own."

Christy, who had been with the company for three years at the time, was a planner in the hydraulics department. She told the OCC that even though she had an accounting degree, playing the Great Game forced her to dust off ideas and concepts she hadn't used since she was in school, especially when it came to forecasting. "It used to be that we would just get our production schedule and we would produce what we were asked to do," she said. "Now we know we need to look at margins as well as sales, knowing that even if we increase sales, we could make less profit. Now we know what to fix, which has been a huge change in our culture. Now we know how we could control our future."

John is an assembler who has worked for the company since he graduated from technical college early in his career. He admitted he was scared when the former owners announced they were going to close the plant down. "I wondered where I was going to go from here," he said. When the company got a lifeline, though, he said it was like a shot in the arm. "It was time to go get it," he said. "It was almost like we had more to prove, now that we had to think smarter to earn our keep."

It also helped that, for the first time in his career, someone was sharing the numbers behind the business. "Now that I have more of an ownership stake," he said, "I'm working harder and listening more than ever before. It makes you think more about what you're doing on a daily basis rather than just showing up and going home. I feel like I'm making a difference."

Greg, the CFO, joined the company after it had embraced the Great Game system. It was Greg's first experience of working for an employee-owned company, and he wondered why he hadn't applied to one sooner. "Ownership makes everyone feel like their ideas and opinions count," Greg said. Just as his colleagues were, Greg was eager to get going with the OCC so that he could teach himself and his associates what their ESOP would mean to their future.

By combining their skills with some new capital and an education in the Great Game system, the team at the factory learned what they needed to go beyond survival. They tackled the challenges with enthusiasm. But they also had to grapple with the uncertainty in the market, just as most of the other companies out there had to. Weathering a recession was nothing new to me—we had gone through four of them during my career—but it was interesting to see how this newly transparent and empowered business would handle this challenge as well as others.

FROM SURVIVING TO THRIVING

The exciting news is that the story of the mining equipment factory continues today, more than ten years after the employees embraced the system. They are now firmly in control of their destiny as they work together to determine the kind of business they want to have today—and into the future. Rather than simply reacting to the market, they are getting ahead of it by collecting economic and competitive data to understand trends in supply and demand at a macro and micro level. They have learned to work together to diversify their business and to find new areas for growth. In short, they have completed a remarkable turnaround, a complete transformation of their culture and the people who drive it. And yet the management team there doesn't feel that their journey is over. They continue to learn and evolve as they embrace the system and use it to continue growing their business, which, in ten years, has doubled the number of people working there.

I took the opportunity to speak to three of the factory's leaders: Rob, the general manager; Adam, the director of sales; and Becky, their materials manager. In particular, I wanted to know how things had changed in their business—and in them—from the days when it was a division of a big corporation until today, when they are a stand-alone entrepreneurial entity. When I asked them these questions, here's what they had to say:

Adam: "The biggest difference to me is that everything feels more freeing and natural now. We have a standup meeting every morning and we talk about what's happening around the shop that day, our production and quality goals, KPIs, and the barriers we're going to face for the day. A decade ago, these meetings seemed forced. Now they've taken on a life of their own and everything just flows."

Rob: "The biggest difference to me is that we now have the mind-set that it is truly our business. We are now the ones setting the strategy. In the beginning, we made some mistakes because we didn't really understand that it was truly our business to run. We had an adjustment to make from working in a top-down environment to a culture where everyone can make a difference."

Adam: "I have a sister-in-law who is a controller for a manufacturing company in Ohio. When I started telling her about our language, and that we talk about things such as variances and overhead absorption, she became enamored with our system. She said even her general manager wouldn't understand those things. Everyone gets it in our business with the exception of only the newest people."

Becky: "When you're learning something new, sometimes you have to be comfortable not knowing the answer. You will never have all the answers, even as a leader. Sometimes you have to depend on your associates to give you the answers. It needs to become comfortable saying to them, 'I don't know, but help me so that I can then help you.' I have learned to ask the questions."

Adam: "Having a common language makes my job so easy in sales. All I need to do is get our customers in front of our employees and they sell for us. Anytime we have a tour of the factory, I find a reason to bring customers onto the shop floor. They are then just blown away by the level of business knowledge our people have. I have brought in executives from big corporations and they don't know what absorption rates or variances are. But our people do. Our people sell the product because of their knowledge of the business. It's something that makes us unique."

Becky: "I actually started eight years ago, after the transition. When I came on, the financial language everyone was speaking was foreign to me. But today everyone in the office and on the shop floor speaks the same language."

Adam: "I also have a cousin who is a Spanish teacher in an elementary school. She uses an immersion approach where they take these kids who are five or six years old, and they just talk Spanish to them all day. It's amazing how quickly they learn the language. I think we do something similar with financial literacy. People come in and hear these words and wonder what's going on. It can be intimidating at first. But when you continue to talk the same way every day, you can't help but learn it. It has become the language that we speak across the entire company. It crosses departments. It helps us work together and helps each of us understand how we contribute to where we are headed, together."

This whole idea of thinking of the Great Game system as an immersion program that teaches a common language is fascinating to me. We are very intentional about our own training programs. We measure how many hours each associate gets. And they're all so smart when we give them the opportunity to learn. We also think it's a competitive advantage because it's a language that is spoken from the shop floor to the executive offices. It brings people together. We knew their world would begin to look different. Something happens.

We asked the team how they felt about not being managed but, instead, being led by the system, which brings freedom from the burden of management. Here's what they had to say:

Rob: "Playing the Great Game does feel freeing, but it took some adjustments for me, as a leader, after spending years in the military. My instinct was to stick my fingers into things that I knew I had experience with. But once I learned to trust our High Involvement Planning process, I learned to let go. It's still hard for me. It's taken me a long time to get where I am, especially because our old culture was all about micromanaging from the top down. My responsibility now is to help the people do their own thing while I focus on the strategy and the big picture. I have learned to keep quiet more and let people act on their own. As a leader, sometimes your instinct is to talk too much. But really, you need to talk less. It feels better to see managers receiving information from their own departments and involving people from the ground floor up."

Becky: "In other companies I have worked at, we would hire twenty to thirty people a year without any idea of how long they would be working there. That doesn't happen here. We are free of that fear. Because we know what the financials tell us, we know we can keep someone when we hire them. We know where we're going."

Adam: "It has been a bit of a struggle for me. Yes, there is more freedom. But there is also more responsibility. While we try to not lay anyone off, it's always scary to go out on the limb of hiring someone. But when you hire the right people, especially the all-stars, you don't have to worry about them doing their job because the system lets them know what they need to do. That takes a huge load off a leader's shoulders. The system also creates star associates. It's contagious and creates a ripple effect. It's an incredible feeling when you get to that level."

> **When you hire the right people, especially the all-stars, you don't have to worry about them doing their job because the system lets them know what they need to do.**

We weren't surprised to hear how this team had evolved over the past decade, especially when it came to people making decisions with the help of their associates through the HIP process. We asked if they had had any idea ten years earlier that they could design their own future. Here's what they replied:

Rob: "Ten years ago, we lived in fear. Then, when the news came that they were going to close the plant, our biggest fear came true. I was financially literate, and I could see that the business wasn't really sustainable. But I felt like I was the only one who did, which gave me a feeling of being alone. I did what I could do to change things. But I didn't have a lot of control. It was a helpless feeling. Now we can truly impact things and look into the future five to seven years out. We have a vision and a strategy to get us there, which has helped us get past our fears. Yes, we are still paranoid about the market and we look over our shoulders. But I was vulnerable about not having all the answers, and I felt comfortable relying on the whole team. I asked them to work together with me to get where we want to go together. They responded by saying, 'How can we help?'"

Adam: "I had read the book *The Great Game of Business* ten years ago. It sounded great. Even after we toured plants that used the system, we were blown away. We thought it would be so cool to do some of that stuff in our plant. When we got the chance to actually play the system in 2009, we thought we knew what to do. And we did when things were going well. But when the financials struggled, we also struggled with the system. What we realized is that sometimes you have to struggle to learn. You sometimes learn the most when you fail. It was a life lesson."

One of the things we remember most about the team at the factory when we first met them was how sharp they all were in terms of their technical skills. What they didn't have were the skills to build a business. I was curious about how playing the system for a decade had changed that equation, especially when it came to things such as learning the importance of diversifying their business away from a single customer and market. Here's what they told us:

Becky: "When I started eight years ago, diversification was a dirty word. People didn't want to change. After all, they only knew how to do one thing. Today, diversification is something everyone wants. People now understand the importance of it."

Adam: "People told us that we couldn't diversify, that we couldn't make products for other customers. We were so engrained in our old patterns. We struggled for the first two years. Things were not working as well as we wanted. People wanted to stay in their comfort zones, and they were comfortable with what they knew how to do. It was hard for them to do something different, so we lost a lot of momentum. They didn't have the confidence to understand the system."

Rob: "We made the mistake of letting people hang around because they had the right technical skills, even though they were no longer a fit to help build the culture we desired. It was like a football team that has a star player who is selfish in a way that is disruptive to the performance of the team. We made the mistake of thinking we had people who couldn't be replaced even though they had become poison to the culture. Finally, we confronted those situations."

Adam: "You get degrees of fear when people do something they're not comfortable with, especially with people who pride themselves on their technical knowledge. That was what the previous culture required. We heard people tell us over and over again how they only wanted to build engines. They didn't want to learn about the business. Things eventually began to change over time. People began to pick up things gradually. It took a while. And then they surprise you with a great question at a point when you didn't think they were paying attention. When they start asking questions, you know you have created the change."

We thought the team was making an interesting point. We don't live in a perfect world. Things change all the time. But when we tell people to do their job and not worry about anything else, they blame everyone else when they can't perform or get their job done. They stick to accountabilities and job descriptions rather than looking at the bigger picture in the company and how they might contribute their innovation or creativity to build a better place. But if your organization doesn't adapt to the changes in the market or the big picture, then people will continue to get frustrated.

Or worse, they could show up for work one day and find a sign there telling them the place is out of business. The solution is to encourage people to think bigger, to appeal to their higher level of intelligence, and get them involved in building the business. When you do that, you'll also get better performance. You can't jam a process down someone's throat. But if you can inspire people to chase a higher goal, then they will ask for processes to help them reach that goal rather than just focusing on completing their task.

> **If you can inspire people to chase a higher goal, then they will ask for processes to help them reach that goal.**

We asked the team how they got their people to shift their focus from their day-to-day tasks to building something bigger, how they got people thinking outside the box. Here's what they told us:

Rob: "Our challenge was to create a culture where our people understood the big picture, as well as how they could individually impact the numbers and help us get there. We also needed people to learn to roll with changes. We asked them to not just put their head down and do their job but to look up and understand how they could contribute to the big picture and really go somewhere together."

Becky: "Today, our people have a much higher level of engagement outside their particular jobs. They have a much better understanding of what other departments are doing, thanks to the system."

Adam: "We now have a plan to diversify our business. People are engaged in helping us get there. That's a big change from ten years ago."

The team now understands the importance of the HIP process. It helps people recognize that there is a long-range plan and strategy for them to participate in creating. HIP is all about setting a target together. Most companies take a long time to get to that point with HIP. Most companies don't plan. In fact, most people don't plan. But HIP is all about setting a target together and then working collectively to get there. To make the process work requires a great deal of communication. In watching this team evolve over the past decade, I have been blown away by their embrace of financial literacy and use of staff meetings—which we call huddles—as a way to train their people on how the numbers on the income statement, balance sheet, and cash flow statement drive their business forward.

We were curious to know how playing the system affected the team's approach to communication. Here's what they said:

Rob: "We didn't have much communication ten years ago. With our former parent company, there might be one annual company-wide meeting. An executive would give us a presentation using a chart none of us could understand. There were never any follow-ups. That chart hung in our break room forever, and it didn't mean anything to us. It was a symbol of how we didn't know what we were doing or what we should talk about. But after the acquisition, we started huddling right away. And now, ten years later, the huddles haven't stopped."

Adam: "I think the biggest change in our communication was that we moved from talking about tactical things to having more strategic discussions in our staff meetings. We shifted from the day-to-day to our one- and five-year goals."

Becky: "We are more system driven today. Rather than backing up the bus over people, we are more focused on talking about the goals we are trying to achieve. It's a higher level of discussion."

Adam: "It relates to tactical versus strategic thinking. You will miss the big picture if you only focus on the day-to-day job. Sometimes it's more important to take a day to tackle financial literacy training, even if it means you might miss your production goals for the day. You need to look at that as an investment that will give you a greater return in the long run. But that's not always an intuitive or obvious solution."

While we have seen the incredible impact that teaching financial and business literacy can have on our people, we have heard from critics who think the Great Game system is just about the numbers. The critics tell us that we don't care about people because we're only concerned with profit and cash flow. What these folks don't understand is that the Great Game system is all about people: it's about unleashing them and giving them all the tools and information to make the kind of life they want for themselves. We wanted to know what the team thought about this kind of criticism of the system.

Becky: "The critics are missing the bigger picture. The numbers are what helps the people and associates to become more involved in building the company. When they know what's going on, they know how to fix it. Knowing the numbers allows them to measure job security. The system is totally people driven. The numbers are just stories about people."

Adam: "I agree, it's all about the bigger picture. It's not just about ourselves; it's about all of us, as a collective. Sometimes we have to make a decision for the greater good, something that is good for the company over an individual. That can be hard for some people to accept. But the numbers help us to diversify and grow rather than shrink and die."

Rob: "Thinking about the huddles, I remember one time that one of the members of our culture committee got up in a huddle, and he just froze. But someone immediately stood up and took over. He was embarrassed, but everyone rallied around him and encouraged him to keep trying. To go outside their comfort zone can be incredibly difficult for some people. But we continue to encourage them to do that. Ultimately, he was able to stand up in front of everyone, and he learned to tell the stories behind the numbers."

> **Ultimately, he was able to stand up in front of everyone, and he learned to tell the stories behind the numbers.**

Adam: "I don't know how many times we have changed our huddles as our people have gotten more sophisticated about understanding the numbers. It's taken on a life of its own. We even have one associate who used to be a skeptic about the system. Now he runs a training program he set up to help our new employees learn our language. He's not an accountant, so he explains everything in common sense financials. He's also a peer, so people are more open to asking questions about things that they don't understand."

Becky: "We have also used our huddles to break down silos in the business. Because we know the numbers, we can better understand the different decisions being made in the business and see how they make financial sense or not. We understand whether something will move the company forward or not. When I first started here, I didn't understand the impact of overhead and its relationship to cost and margins. Everyone helped me make the connection. But through our huddle rhythm and everyone's help, I eventually got it. Now I am the one helping our new people there too."

In the subsidiaries of our business, our younger associates seem to be picking things up faster than I have ever seen before, including the time when I was a millennial-aged foreman. We asked the team if they saw similar trends in the younger members of their workforce.

Rob: "Yes, we are seeing that our younger employees really embrace the system. Their generation wants to have meaning and to be part of something in their job. The Great Game system connects them to that. Our mission statement is that we want our employees to have a better life. It's why we exist. A lot goes into that, including making money. But creating a better life for themselves is a message that young people can get behind. It's a powerful why."

Adam: "We also use our education programs to promote ownership. I recall one associate who took the lead on getting a discount on tickets to a big basketball game in town. He asked me how much he could spend. I told him it was his budget; he could decide. I told him he could figure it out. He took that and ran with it. He made the decisions, which helped him feel like the owner that he is. It's learning by doing, which is the best teacher."

Becky: "Just the other day I had a guy in our warehouse, a

certified forklift driver, come up to me with a suggestion. He knew we were buying a new truck to help us transport materials. You don't need a special license or training to drive the new truck, but it is different than driving a regular truck. On his own he came up with the idea to have a training program to help people practice so they could avoid accidents. Maybe we wouldn't need it, but he thought it wouldn't hurt. Again, he did that on his own initiative."

Rob: "There's no way people would have taken the initiative ten years ago. Another example is how one of our associates created an ESOP training program on his own. He is super-passionate about this issue. I thought it was a risky idea, but I let him run with it. I needed to let him ride with it and, if it didn't work out, then take accountability for it. But people loved it. It worked out great. And he became a better employee-owner as a result."

Adam: "To make this system work, you have to learn to let go a lot. That's hard for most people, especially if you have been trained your whole life in a command-and-control system. When you're the leader, everyone looks to you. But to lead, you need to let go and let people learn from mistakes."

Becky: "We're hearing more and more people tell us they love to work at our company. They also say they could never work at any other place that doesn't operate this way. When people leave, they want to come back."

Rob: "We have had boomerang situations. We had one associate leave, and a few weeks later, she called back and said she had made a terrible mistake in leaving. She had taken a job to be closer to home. But the company was run by command and control, and she immediately knew she couldn't work there. I love welcoming people like that back. It's like they finally learn what we have here, and they appreciate it in a whole new way. They realize that they are getting something of value with our culture, something they can take home as well."

Adam: "It's not just the language; it's the whole system that they value. It goes back to HIP. We sit together and come up with our own annual plans. When we put a bonus plan together, we see if the numbers work out or not. It gets back to the sense of freedom we have. The language is how you communicate, but the system is what ties us all together. That's how we have created our transformation."

One final question we asked was, If this system is so great, why isn't everyone doing it?

Rob: "I think it's because most people don't believe it can work. I was in a local Vistage group for about five years, and most of those business owners were skeptical about their employees knowing about the business. They didn't want confidential business information getting out and they didn't believe their employees had the capacity to learn about business."

Adam: "I think the barrier for most people is that it's too hard to let go of control. It's a natural tendency for many of us to want control, which means you worry about everything. You don't trust people enough to let them screw up. You need to tell them what to do and how to do it. That's why embracing the system is so freeing compared to keeping control. But most people don't get that."

Rob: "People who reject this system do so because they're not willing to give information to their employees. They don't have confidence that their people will learn this."

Becky: "And they don't want to take the time to teach them, because a lot of the owners don't know it themselves. They don't understand the financials. They rely on their accountants and lawyers to tell them."

Rob: "It does help to have the support and guidance of a community of experts like we have with the Great Game. I don't know if we could have done what we have without them. There are so many people that have acted as guide posts for us over the past ten years. We're excited to see where we can go in the next ten years and beyond—and the system will help us get there."

CHAPTER THREE

AN AMERICAN BUSINESS TRAGEDY

The statistics tell us that most companies never make it past their five-year anniversary. That's a tragedy. What a tremendous waste of money and people's time and effort. But any business can fail at any time, even companies with decades of success. The Great Game system is designed to help prevent these tragedies, which is why we constantly look for opportunities to teach other organizations about how the system works.

One way we do that is by encouraging people in our company to join for-profit and nonprofit boards. I have heard plenty of people suggest that companies shouldn't let people waste their time volunteering. But we have found that when we let our people go out and see how good or bad it can be in other organizations, they come back as better leaders who bring more energy, information, and knowledge of best practices back to the Great Game.

Take Ron, for example. He is one of the executives at SRC who volunteers on various nonprofit boards in our community. Ron's been working at SRC since our International Harvester days in the late 1970s. In his thirty-five years at SRC, he's learned the art of peeking around corners into the future while also covering his tracks with plenty of trap doors and contingency plans. More importantly, Ron always meets his plans. He's someone who understands the transformative power of playing the Great Game.

One day, Ron walked into my office. He wanted to tell me a story about a company board he had joined a year earlier. It was a manufacturing company he knew through their mutual involvement in a statewide association. When Ron joined the board, the company had completed a succession: the founder had stepped away from the business after selling it to his 150 employees through an ESOP.

Ron was specifically interested in learning how a succession in an ESOP company worked so he could bring that knowledge back to SRC. Ron was also interested in joining the board because the guy who was taking over as president of the company said he wanted to teach financial literacy to everyone in the business, which Ron knew was an essential component of creating informed owners such as those we have at SRC. It's been part our mantra for a long time that equity is not a magic pill and that ownership needs to be taught.

Based on everything he knew up-front, it seemed to Ron that the company, which had been around for forty years, had all the right ingredients to continue to be an outrageous success. Ownership was shared with the employees. The product was in massive demand: top-line sales were through the roof at more than $30 million. The owner-employees even had a big, audacious vision of becoming the leaders in the industry.

When Ron came into my office, he was beyond upset. It was as if he were going to a confessional. Rather than watching the company take off, Ron had a front-row seat to witnessing the company head off a cliff. "Jack," he said, "I've never seen anything go south as quickly as this company did."

The company was mired in debt, losing money, and in violation of its banking covenants, and its vendors were threatening to hold all shipments until they were paid. Despite its long track record of success, the company suddenly faced the very real threat of going out of business because it had committed the deadliest sin in business: it had run out of cash. As Ron continued to talk, I wondered if I were about to hear another chapter in the great American business tragedy.

Ron mentioned the things he could have done differently over the past year and that he should have spotted the mounting red flags that signaled the kind of death spiral the company had fallen into. The more of Ron's story I heard, the clearer the key to all of the company's problems became: the company's president was stuck in an old school, top-down mind-set.

SUCCESSION PLANNING GONE WRONG

Ron began his story by telling me that he knew the factory's founder, a veteran military engineer, whom Ron would meet at manufacturing association meetings they both attended for many years. The founder invented a product, around which he built a successful company.

When the founder turned sixty-five, he began thinking about retiring at the age of seventy.

Since he didn't have any family members interested in taking over the business from him, the founder began building a succession plan that would help ensure that the business and its employees remained rooted in the community.

The first step the founder took was to hire, from outside the company, a talented young executive whom he could train to take over running the business when he was gone. The founder then spent the next five years grooming the new president. His intention was to teach him everything he had learned about running the business over the previous four decades. The founder sold the business to his employees through an ESOP even though that meant he would be selling the company at a lower valuation than he might have received from a strategic or financial buyer.

In building his company over the years, the founder had, remarkably, never taken on any debt. When it came to selling the business to his employees, he didn't want to force the company to take on debt just to buy him out. He agreed to be paid off over a ten-year period during which he would serve as chairman of the board of directors to keep an eye on his baby. While the company still had the financial liability of paying off the founder, it didn't have to borrow money. It would pay him off over the planned period of ten years, using cash flow as its source of funds.

The founder believed he had checked all the right boxes when it came to putting together an airtight succession plan. Five years later, Ron joined the board. Before joining, he was advised that the note owed to the founder had been paid off five years earlier than the plan called for, with the approval of the board. The succession plan had sprung a leak.

He learned that the president, who had taken over running the company five years earlier, had decided it was time for the founder to move on. The president wanted more autonomy to make decisions without having to get the founder's approval at board meetings. He had the company take on debt to pay off the founder earlier than planned and get the founder off the board.

Even though the founder was willing to take a little less by selling to the ESOP, the company was still worth several million dollars. That meant the company had now taken on a substantial liability for the first time in its history.

When Ron asked the founder why he had agreed to adjust the pay-out plan, he told Ron that since he had taught the president everything he knew, he didn't want to stand in his successor's way. He wanted to give him the chance to build his own legacy. He hoped the company could be even more successful under the new president's leadership.

Looking back with the benefit of hindsight, Ron could see clearly that taking on debt to pay off the founder was the first serious warning sign that the company was headed down the road to trouble. After all, learning to live with debt was not a lesson the founder had taught the president, who was breaking new ground on his own. One of the tragedies of succession planning is that company founders don't teach their people the intricacies of the game they are playing.

Ron knew all about the perils of owing money. Paying off our debt was the very first critical number in the early days of SRC, which Ron had experienced firsthand. At that time, every single person in the company knew that if we ran out of cash, we were dead in the water. That's a powerful lesson debt teaches you, and it's why we learned to hate it.

We still act that way. Every single day, the first thing we do is check the cash position of each of SRC's business units, as do all the executives who report to me. It's that important.

In the case of this factory, Ron was new to the board, and he was reluctant to come to any hasty conclusions. But he wanted to learn more about how this president ran his operation before he sounded any alarms.

Ron saw the next red flag when the company's CFO sent out the quarterly reports to each member of the board. As Ron began looking at the statements, he immediately spotted something alarming: the company was not hitting its plan. Not only were the sales numbers coming in under their projections, but the company was spending far more on capital investments than the plan called for. What was going on?

At SRC meetings, all personnel are encouraged to speak up when they have questions, especially when it comes to a deviation in the financials. We hold each other accountable when we're off plan and offer suggestions for how to fix things. Whenever we speak up and ask what went wrong, we also offer whatever help someone might need to get back on plan or to create a solution to help solve the problem.

Ron called the president. "You're missing your earnings and cash flow projections," he said, "and your debt is creeping up. Why?"

The president explained to Ron that the company had made several major capital investments, including purchasing a new building and replacing old machinery with new high-tech equipment. They also had spent a great deal of money installing a new software system to speed their ordering and inventory processes. The company had taken on debt to fund all of these investments, in addition to all the other debt taken on to pay the founder's note.

Now that the company was missing its projections, Ron questioned the president about whether the company's bank would be worried about the health of the company's cash flow. He mentioned that an overlooked secret of successful businesses is that they have learned to say no to opportunities that are wrong for them. Ron also reminded the president that since the company was an ESOP, he couldn't afford to have any cash problems, given the obligations the company had to employee-owners who were nearing retirement. Ron suggested that the president send a report to the rest of the board, pointing out where the company had missed its projections, why they had happened, and what he was going to do to get back on plan.

To his credit, the president was very respectful of Ron. He said he was glad to get the input. He also said he'd have his CFO get back to Ron with the reasons behind the deviations. His tone of voice exuded confidence (as in "Trust me. I've got this").

About a week later, the CFO emailed Ron with a cursory explanation for the missed projections. He wrote that everything was going to get back on track by the end of the second quarter. The CFO didn't elaborate on exactly how that was going to happen, which sounded a full-scale alarm in Ron's head.

Ron had also noticed that the company had a strange way of paying off people when they left the company and the ESOP. Rather than paying the employee over a period of a few years, the company paid them on the same day they left it. The company would buy out the employees' shares in the ESOP and put their proceeds in an interest-bearing money market fund. The employees would be paid out of that account for the next five years.

But that was a lose-lose process for the company and the employees. The company was losing the cash up-front and the employees were earning a minuscule amount of interest on their money during one of the hottest markets in years.

Ron suggested that the company make a change. They should purchase the employees' shares over a five-year period, which would free up, in the short term, substantial cash that he hoped the president would use to pay down some of the company's mounting debt.

That turned out to be wishful thinking on Ron's part.

A SLIPPERY SLOPE

Ron knew that everyone in the company was excited about the company's trajectory, including the other board members. But he didn't understand why the board had approved some of the decisions the president had made over the previous few years. Why had they allowed him to take on all that debt by buying out the founder? Maybe they believed they would simply grow out of their debt? As a veteran of playing the Game, Ron knew better than that.

He could also see the signs that the company's cash position was unraveling by the day. But what was his obligation, as a board member, other than to point out the warning signs?

After the third quarter ended, the board got back together, this time at a lakeside cabin. As the meeting got started, waiters began serving fancy food and drinks. To Ron, everything felt more like a party than a board meeting.

When the president got around to his presentation, he didn't hand out any financial statements. Rather, he began painting a picture of where he was taking the company, using a new set of projections. All he talked about were his ideas for the future and where the numbers were headed. It was an inspiring vision, but one that lacked any substance.

The president promised that all of the investments the company had funded through its debt were about to pay off, big time. "This guy could sell ice to Eskimos," Ron told me. "He was so optimistic. He seemed to really believe in what he was saying even though he wasn't using facts or spreadsheets to make his case."

To Ron, it seemed that the president was always selling his dream of the future while ignoring the reality of the present. He truly believed in the vision he was presenting, but he didn't have a plan for getting there. This is the essence of the tragedy. The company didn't need the new building and wouldn't be able to fully utilize it for another twenty-four months, according to the president's plan. The board had approved the purchase, based on the previous projections the president had given them, but no contingency plans were in place should the company fail to make its cash flow budget. Worse, the projections weren't based on legal commitments such as purchase orders, contracts, and customer commitments. He was flying by the seat of his pants and making projections using his gut.

> He truly believed in the vision he was presenting, but he didn't have a plan for getting there.

Another warning sign was that several key, long-term employees—including several managers—had left the company or taken early retirement. When Ron asked the president why turnover had jumped, the president chalked it up to personal issues or competitors trying to poach their best people. It wasn't anything to worry about, the president said. He'd take care of it.

MISSED OPPORTUNITIES

"Maybe that meeting was my missed opportunity," Ron told me, beating himself up a bit. "The fact that the president hadn't even reported the actual results from the quarter should have alarmed every one of us board members into taking action."

That never would have happened at SRC. We work with our financials in real-time and through our constant huddling, not to mention our bi-annual HIP meetings where all of our divisions get together to compare our progress on achieving our plans and forecasts. Paranoia can be good for you—unless you don't do something about what scares you. You can't hide from the solution and be successful.

Our forecasts are also much more than projections. Just giving someone a quote on an order wouldn't count toward a forecast at SRC. Our people would throw rotten eggs at people who rely only on their gut. We need a purchase order or a supply agreement—an actual commitment—before we believe it. We know we can't rely on fluff and speculation, especially when we have to share those forecasts with hundreds of our fellow employee-owners in one of our HIP sessions—and explain how we came up with them in the first place. We have to substantiate our sales. The more checks and balances you have, the more accurate your forecasts become. Contingency planning is also the art of minimizing risk while understanding that risk is also unavoidable. If you want to succeed in business, you need to be willing to deal with the unexpected and be prepared for it.

We see these HIP meetings as our opportunities to teach our people that the goals the company needs to meet are set by the market, not just dreamed up by management. And it's magical to see that light bulb go off when someone begins to understand why those goals exist, and how they, personally, can affect them. People begin to understand why certain decisions get made, how the company makes or loses money, and what the company does with its earnings. The mistake most people make is that they focus only on the profit, not where the profit goes or where it's most needed. Don't milk the cow until it runs out of milk. Sometimes you need to go back and feed the cow.

When you involve your people in planning for the future, they can also help develop the kind of diversified product and service that can serve as your contingency plans and trap doors you can fall back on if the markets or projections turn against you. We want to build the kind of joint accountability and alignment that ensures everyone is pulling together toward our shared goals. All of our people vote on our plan, which means that our company can't be run by one leader relying on personal gut decisions. All our leaders are held in check by transparency and accountability.

We've also learned that the more you teach people about financials, the smarter and more conservative they get with the company's money because they begin to think of it as *their* money. The paradox here is that so many business owners complain that employees don't think as they do. "Why can't my people think more like owners

The more you teach people about financials, the smarter and more conservative they get with the company's money because they begin to think of it as *their* money.

when it comes to spending money?" they might say. But what they miss is the chance to tap into the wisdom of the crowd. The lynchpin of the Great Game system is having the eyes and brains of our associates involved with every aspect of running the business. We want to appeal to the highest level of thinking in our people.

But Ron's company was not transparent with its financials. It wasn't open at all. There was a veil of secrecy keeping people in the company from the facts that would help determine whether their organization was winning or losing. The president held the keys to all of the information.

"He knew how to read financials," Ron told me. "But he decided not to believe them. He was only willing to share the numbers he wished were true. If they had actually been reporting from the bottom up, they might have known what was going to happen to them much sooner."

RED ALERT

The alarm bells sounded in earnest one day in November when a purchasing manager got a call from one of the company's suppliers. The supplier was outraged. He wanted to know why the factory was so late in paying him for previous orders. His invoices were now more than ninety days outstanding. He was threatening to stop shipping product until he got paid.

The message from the supplier was shocking news to the purchasing manager. He hadn't known anything about it. He was always told to just do his job and not worry about paying the bills. But when he started talking to a few of his peers about the call, he learned that there were other vendors who weren't being paid either. Something had obviously gone wrong.

That was seriously bad news because the factory relied on a relatively quick turnaround from its suppliers. It placed orders just forty-five days out from where those supplies were needed in production. If the shipments from the vendors stopped, the company would collapse like a house of cards. What those employee-owners on the front lines had just learned was that the president had leveraged his payables and stretched his vendors because he had run out of credit everywhere else. Living off your payables is the last foot to the grave. It shows that you have exhausted your entire supply of cash and debt.

It came out later that some of the employees had left because they were worried the company wasn't doing as well financially as the president told them it was. There were whispers among the employee-owners that they could lose everything in their ESOP accounts. The people knew something was wrong. They always do.

When managers don't share the financials or teach their people how the financials can affect them, people make up their own answers.

More often than not, they are the wrong answers. But people often know that something is wrong even if they're not told. As we always say at SRC, you can fool the fans, but you can't fool the players.

The purchasing manager was a longtime employee, and he had the founder's phone number. So he called the founder to let him know what had happened with the supplier and shed some light on the recent turnovers. He also let the founder know that everyone was concerned about the value of the company.

When the founder hung up the phone, he was stunned. He called the board members, who, after hearing the news, convened an emergency board meeting at which the president was asked to report on the status of the financials. This included explaining how he was tracking progress in hitting the company's goals for the year. Because the board members also wanted convincing explanations for the deviations in the plan, the president had to bring the actual financial statements, not simply projections.

When Ron and the others saw the actual numbers, they were shocked by how bad things had become. The company had been missing its targets for months. Worse, they were rapidly running out of cash, which was why the suppliers weren't being paid. The company was also dangerously close to violating its covenants with its bank, which meant it wouldn't be able to make the payments against its debt as promised.

That's not something you want to surprise your bank with. If you break a covenant with a bank, the best case is that the bank will raise your interest rate. It's just as likely that the bank will freeze your line of credit or, worse case, call in the loan, which is truly the end of the line. Game over.

Even if the turnaround the president predicted had come about, he probably wouldn't have had enough cash on hand to save the company. For all the lessons the founder had tried to teach him, the lesson they never covered concerned the dangers of debt. Now it looked as if his addiction to debt would sink the company.

When the board questioned the president about the shaky financial state of the business, he used the same defense he had used earlier in the year: it was just a deviation and things would get back on track during the next quarter.

This time, Ron's fellow board members weren't convinced. They demanded to see, within the next thirty days, an updated budget for the coming year as well as the president's plan for turning things around.

EYES WIDE OPEN

A month later, when the president presented the current budget to the board, there was a lot of skepticism, especially from Ron: the numbers still seemed far too flowery and optimistic to be true. There was no market or operational data to back them up either.

He also didn't have any recovery or contingency plan in place. He hadn't thought at all about what would happen if the company didn't make its plan or what the company would do if it couldn't meet its debt obligations. "I can't approve this budget," Ron told the president. "I want the real numbers. I don't trust you anymore."

Prior to that meeting, Ron and the other board members had met exclusively with the president in their board meetings. Now, they asked the chief financial officer and the rest of the management team to come in and explain where the various departmental budget numbers came from.

It quickly became evident that the management had been strong-armed by the president into making up numbers that had no basis in the market, no credibility. This is the mortal sin of top-down forecasts.

The president had locked himself in a room and made up the story. They were running the company on numbers the president merely hoped they could make. It's easy to imagine how lonely he had become, how afraid he was, thinking that the entire company's fortunes rested on his shoulders alone. But he also didn't want to hear what anyone else had to say. Big mistake.

"He was presenting the board with false projections," Ron told me. "He was presenting hunches. And as things got worse, the less he shared. But he had reached a point where he couldn't hide anymore. If anything, I was shocked the CFO hadn't called the board about this earlier."

As the board continued to dissect the numbers, it suddenly dawned on everyone that even though the president's plan projected $2 million in profit, the company would actually lose money for the first time in its long history. That meant that while cash outflows were already out of control, now the cash inflows were down, which spelled disaster. They were truly out of cash.

As a result of that meeting, the board could now see that the company was in violation of its bank covenants. The board's eyes had finally been opened to the very real threat that the company might have to shut its doors, crushing the hopes and dreams of 150 families who were the reason the founder started the company in the first place.

At that point the board knew what had to be done: they had to fire the president and find a new source of money immediately to try and save those jobs.

ONE STEP BACK, TWO STEPS FORWARD

That was an emotional day for Ron, and all of those final meetings happened over the holidays. It was something he never wanted to

73

experience again. "The guy wasn't evil," Ron told me. "He was a nice guy and his heart was in the right place. He truly believed that everything was about to turn around."

But rather than share the truth of the situation, the president continued to pull away from the board. He began hiding numbers and then making them up to stall and buy time for his plan to kick in. The worse things got, the more he turned inward rather than asking for help. In that sense, he betrayed all of his fellow employee-owners. He thought he was sparing them from the truth, somehow protecting them, rather than getting them on board to right the ship by working together.

Ron said letting the president go was also hard on the founder. After all, he had groomed his successor for several years. "The founder wondered what he missed about the guy," Ron told me. How did things get so off track? He had a good vision for the company, but he didn't have the ability to make the money to fund it in a realistic timeframe. "It was like giving a teenager the keys to a car for the first time," Ron told me. "He just wanted to take off. It was all ambition with no financial discipline. He didn't understand the financial basics of business."

Maybe the founder's real missed opportunity was that having a succession plan in place wasn't the same as developing a financial and business literacy program aimed at the entire organization.

After Ron and the board fired the president, they sat down with groups of the hourly associates—three or four at a time—to explain what had happened. And if there was one reaction common to everyone with whom he talked, it was relief. People were thankful to finally know what was really going on even if the news was grim. That's why there is power in being open and honest with your people.

They hadn't received actual numbers on the business's progress in years, which only fed their wildest nightmares of what was really happening. By hiding the truth from them, the president had missed out on tapping into their energy and creative solutions to finding a way out of the hole he had dug. They would have helped him avoid the hole in the first place. They would have asked why the company was borrowing so much money. The organization missed the chance to tap its people for help in developing diversified products and services that could serve as contingency plans and trap doors they could rely on should the market turn against them or their forecast turn out to be wrong.

When you don't share information, you leave people disconnected. As a result, they might not even realize they are causing damage to their department, or the company's bottom line. How can a company's key performance indicators or management by objectives—the metrics the management pays attention to—be expected to tie to an income statement or a balance sheet when you've hidden those financial scorecards from everyone? So many smart people miss the fact that opening the books and sharing the financial picture of the company—good or bad—doesn't scare people off. In fact, it eliminates misperceptions. What is gained instead is the enormous opportunity to get people on board with fixing problems. You can create buy-in by sharing bad news.

Since the president controlled everything, there were no lines of communication to keep everyone working in alignment, which led to inefficiencies and missed opportunities rather than the growth the president kept predicting. So the organization quickly began to wobble out of balance—and out of cash.

Now that they knew the truth, the associates at the factory were scared but also committed to turning things around. As another one of our higher laws states, it's easy to stop one guy, but it's pretty hard to stop one hundred.

A HAPPY ENDING

A few months later, I walked down the hallway into Ron's office. I wanted to get an update on where things stood with the factory. "Did they have to close their doors?" I asked Ron.

"Thankfully, no," he told me. "But it was close."

The board brought in an interim president with experience in the industry and scrambled to repair relationships with the company's lenders. The founder had to put about $750,000 back into the company as a bridge loan to keep operations going, money he wouldn't get back unless the company turned itself around.

The banks were willing to keep working with the company as long as it had a realistic budget and projections for the next year. Banks will work with you if they believe you are telling them the truth.

To build that trust, Ron and the board enlisted the help of the company's employee-owners to create their own budgets and forecasts for the first time. They also set up a rigorous weekly schedule that now involved everyone in the company in tracking how the company was performing relative to its goals. This included paying off debt and all the vendors. Cash was going to be tight for the next few months, maybe years, but there would be no more surprises.

The good news was that, thanks to the help of a Great Game veteran, the company had a solution to the problem before it was too late. It didn't become just another chapter in the great American business tragedy—and another statistic in the failure column. When you finally realize that it's the hoarding of information that can kill your company, then you can unlock the door to creating a sustainable success story over the long run.

We're going to see more and more tragedies like this in the years ahead because our young entrepreneurs aren't learning about the destructive power of debt. They're being taught to think and act as the former president of that manufacturing company did, which should serve as a big wake-up call for all the universities and business incubators that are spreading this misinformation.

CHAPTER FOUR
WHAT ARE WE TEACHING ENTREPRENEURS THESE DAYS?

U nfortunately, it's not just decades-old companies that hoard information or run out of cash. It happens to companies of all shapes and sizes every day. And sometimes they're even being told it's good for their business. If that sounds crazy to you, you're right. It's crazy. And what about schools and innovation centers that teach a generation of young entrepreneurs what they need to do to succeed but don't include classes on managing cash?

We learned the following lesson from Doug, a serial entrepreneur and author who now teaches entrepreneurship classes to college students. Doug told me about the first class he taught and that he started it with a question. He asked his students what the definition of *profit* was. To guide them, he offered two possible definitions:

- **Definition 1: profit represents value.**

- **Definition 2: profit represents cheating the customer.**

When Doug asked for a show of hands for each definition, he was shocked to see that about 60 percent of the students chose the second definition. He knew then that he had a lot of ground to cover that semester to explain what profit really was. At the same time, Doug began informally polling other people by asking them the same question—at conferences and cocktail parties—and he found that they, too, chose the second definition more than half the time. He began to wonder if there was something in the water. Why did people think profit was such a bad thing?

In the fifteen years since then, Doug has continued to start every semester with that same question. Incredibly, he found that he got roughly the same response every time. It got him worried about the future and what kids were learning. What stunned him the most was that these were *business students* who were answering the question this way. Doug eventually coauthored an article that was published in a prominent academic journal. The article reported the results of his surveys and suggested they might be indicative of a knowledge gap in today's society about what profit is and what it's used for.

To me, it's a clear indicator that people, especially young people, aren't being taught the rules, and they're putting their lives, let alone their businesses, at risk. I've witnessed this trend firsthand. One great example is that of Jesse, a bright young woman who happened to know me through one of my daughters. Jesse and her husband, Sam, had started an e-commerce site in 2013, which they were operating out of a business incubator based near a major university. The business had an interesting niche in that it catered to home designers and renovators, and interest in the business was booming. She had heard that

I had made some angel investments in young companies like hers, so Jesse called me up one day in hopes that I would be willing to review and possibly invest in their venture.

During that phone call, I learned that both Jesse and Sam had run businesses of their own. Jesse had a ton of experience in the marketing world as well as interior decorating and design. Sam, who had graduated from college with a degree in finance, had been working in the banking industry for several years, where he had been part of several mortgage company start-ups. It was clear they already had a lot of combined entrepreneurial experience.

It was also hard to ignore the passion in Jesse's voice when she explained what her business did and where she wanted to take it. The idea had come from the fact that Jesse's friends and family kept asking for advice on how they could remake their homes. But whenever Jesse went to buy any supplies, she was forced to pay marked-up retail prices; she couldn't get access to better wholesale deals because she was just an independent contractor. Her business idea was based on selling products, supplies, and designs to other design contractors at reasonable prices. It seemed an interesting concept, so I agreed to meet with Jesse and Sam to learn more about how they were building their business.

Just a few minutes into our conversation, I immediately knew something was wrong. Jesse and Sam's pitch was entirely aimed at raising money in exchange for an equity stake in their business. All they talked about was how much they thought the premoney valuation of their business was. What was missing was any real discussion about how they would earn a profit and generate cash. So, when they told me they thought their business was worth more than $2 million, based purely on the advice they had been given, I just about had a coronary. They were evaluating their company based on potential alone.

When I looked at their financials and their projections, the story only got worse; there were red flags everywhere. It was like looking at a business plan from outer space. Early on, they had done a good job of managing their expenses—they had broken even in their first year—which their coaches at the incubator told them was an amazing accomplishment. But things then went downhill. Their coaches told them they were in a hot industry and had to outgrow their competitors if they wanted to be successful over the long term. Jesse and Sam were coached to model themselves after a neighboring business in the incubator that was now planning a move to New York City after that business had landed a superhigh valuation by investors.

Jesse and Sam wanted to ramp things up. They wanted to spend more and more money by hiring employees and investing incredible sums in their marketing campaigns. They had started the business with their savings, but they planned to quickly increase their spending after they secured a $50,000 loan from the Small Business Administration.

What I couldn't get my head around was how much they wanted to spend on online marketing and advertising: thousands of dollars a month. I had never seen another business in which sales and marketing expenses were more than 20 percent of their sales. But projected marketing expenses for these kids accounted for 90 percent of their cost of goods sold. In other words, most of the costs of running their business would be tied up in buying online advertising to try to win new customers.

"We constantly kept tabs on what our larger competitors were doing and how much they were growing," Sam told me. "We kept spending more to try to keep up with them. We really wanted to push and scale up as fast as we could."

"We had our eyes on the prize," Jesse said.

What they didn't realize was that they had entered an unsustainable rat race they couldn't hope to win by trying to spend as much as they could in online advertising. When you have to spend all your money up-front just to get customer leads that only have the promise of future revenue, you'll burn through your cash faster than you could ever imagine. They didn't realize they were caught up in what was as close to a Ponzi scheme as I'd ever seen. They'd been brainwashed to believe that everything revolves around social media sites such as Facebook and Instagram. They fell into the trap of running their business based solely on the notion of how many hits their website got or where they were placed in a search result. They had to invest more and more money to stay ahead of their competitors on search results. But those competitors were also using the same strategy, so they were engaged in an arms race that would likely lead to mutually assured destruction. The social media companies would make out just fine no matter what happened.

> **But those competitors were also using the same strategy, so they were engaged in an arms race that would likely lead to mutually assured destruction.**

I know that's part of running the business these days, but it's not the whole big picture. And what happened is these kids ended up spending all their time trying to figure that part out and were not focused enough on building and running their business. They didn't know the rules.

If they followed their plan, they would outrun their coverage by spending too much, too fast, which would leave them in a disastrous position. It was clear to me they were going to soon face a severe cash crunch. They would go through every circle of Dante's hell to acquire money to grow their business. But why? They didn't realize that path would suck all the oxygen out of their bodies, as well as their children's, and they could lose their house. If they didn't land an investor willing to put money into the business, they might not even survive the year. But even if they were to secure some cash in the short term, I wasn't convinced they could execute their long-term vision, especially if they had to answer to an outside investor. Most people overlook how devastating debt is. It erodes security and protection in a way that makes people do crazy things.

Despite the fact that these two young people had a couple of young kids at home, they were ready to mortgage their house and everything they had to make their business a success. I really wanted to help them—but only if they were willing to learn there was a better way to run their business.

They were focused more on creating a million-dollar company than they were on putting food on the table or being able to go home after work and watching their kids play basketball. They didn't realize how much time they would spend meeting with their investors and explaining how they were going to hit their numbers. Many failed entrepreneurs think they can grow out of their problems. They need to learn to do more with less instead.

So I asked them, "Why are you doing it this way? Why are you so focused on bringing in outside investors to grow so fast? Don't you want to raise your family and have a life?"

Jesse and Sam explained that it was their mentors and other startup entrepreneurs at the incubator who told them this was the way they needed to build their business. Their advisers wanted them to outrun their competition. But did their teachers also explain the kinds of emotional strings that come attached to borrowing money? I think there is a big cognitive gap here. Sam and Jesse didn't realize that misery and pain goes along with borrowing money from outside investors. They were not aware they would have sleepless nights worrying about whether they could make their payroll and whether they would let down the people who lent them the money. It can be a horrific experience. Just picture yourself in a situation where you've borrowed money from your parents' retirement account, and you can't pay them back. It is why debt can become a suffocating black hole.

Apparently, they had been scouring the country, traveling multiple times to cities such as New York, Saint Louis, and Kansas City in search of investors willing to back their venture. Having struck out to that point, they were now expanding their search by talking to potential investors on the West Coast as well. "We had such a strong vision for what we wanted to build," said Jesse. "But we were frustrated because it didn't seem like we could get traction with investors. We didn't know why we couldn't get them to see our vision."

I was stunned. It was clear to me that despite their experience in running businesses, they couldn't even spell *equity*. Their coaches had somehow convinced them that building an internet-based business was different, that the old rules of building a business needed to be thrown out in favor of something new tied to the internet. It was as if the dot-com era was happening all over again.

The truth was, however, that they were being taught to fail. While that might sound harsh, I was completely baffled by the fact that these young entrepreneurs believed their ultimate goal was to have investors value their business as highly as possible and then scale up as fast as they could to be able, eventually, to pay off those investors. They might even be forced to sell their business, something that wasn't part of their long-term plan.

What really angers me is that this same model is being taught to a generation of entrepreneurs through schools and so-called incubators and innovation centers that supposedly exist to nurture and support young businesses. But to what end? That's why most companies never make it past their fifth anniversary.

What I can't understand is why people are in a rush to give away so much of the equity in their company to an outside investor if it isn't necessary. They are, essentially, buying bosses who will climb on their backs and drive every decision they need to make. They will work the same number of hours to grow the business, but the upside won't belong to them any longer; it will be the outside investors who reap the benefits of the entrepreneurs' hard work.

It's as if the tried-and-true rules of running a business are being forgotten in favor of something else. But the financials don't lie. They are your guides to understanding how fast you can grow. Today's entrepreneurs are being taught to ignore those facts. Something like only 10 percent of companies reach the $1 million revenue mark. And yet so many young business entrepreneurs are encouraged to race against each other to build the next Amazon or Facebook, and this advice is killing companies and wasting a lot of capital as a result.

I really liked Jesse and Sam. They had grit. But that put me in a tough position. It was clear that without an infusion of cash, their company would soon be on its last legs, maybe in less than ninety days. Yet I felt they didn't need an investor as much as they needed someone to give them a practical education.

While they wanted me to consider giving them some money in exchange for an equity stake in the company, I didn't want to take the direct investment route. Instead, I offered to loan them unsecured money at a superlow interest rate they could then use as collateral to go back to their bank and get a larger loan. I did some homework on their financials and came up with an amount I figured would help them right their ship. Because the loan was unsecured, I knew most banks would be willing to lend up to three or four times that amount because, if something were to go wrong in the business, the banks would get first dibs on reimbursement.

Before I lent Jesse and Sam the money, they had to make some changes in their business model. That started with addressing the company killer staring them right in the face: lack of cash flow. They faced a fundamental problem in that their vendors had asked them to pay cash for all their products at the time they ordered them. But they wouldn't receive any money from their customers for some thirty or sixty days after they shipped the product to them. It was an unsustainable model unless they could get better terms from vendors they could pay later, preferably after their customers had paid them.

They were also planning to move the business into a new location, but I told them the cost of the new building would put even more pressure on their cash flow.

I think they were surprised, maybe even disappointed, by my decision. But I really wanted them to learn what it meant to run their business rather than just run around looking to hand their company over to investors. I had walked away from making investments before, unless the entrepreneurs were willing to listen and transform their way of thinking about their business. I wanted Jesse and Sam to learn how to grow slow and smart. I wanted them to borrow money to help grow the business, not go out of business by continuing to dump their cash into a bottomless pit. They wanted to have this fast-growth internet company. I wanted them to grow out of their house. Rather than becoming their angel investor, I was hoping to serve as their guardian angel.

As we talked through my plan, I could see Jesse and Sam's eyes opening. And to their credit, they jumped into making changes to deal with their challenges.

Just a few months later, they had a lot of exciting updates to share with me.

They had successfully negotiated better terms with seven of their top ten suppliers. They also called up their credit card company and asked for extended payment terms so they could pay their bill in forty-five to sixty days instead of thirty, which also gave their cash flow some much-needed breathing room.

They went to work on managing their expenses better. They slashed their monthly marketing budget basically in half. They also scrapped the plan to move to the new office they were considering, which would have cost $7 a square foot plus the added cost of building out the space to their needs. After some research, they found another option with a landlord who offered them office space at $2 a square foot.

Jesse and Sam learned from negotiating with their suppliers that they could get better pricing—as much as a 10 percent discount— if they had a brick-and-mortar retail location. Apparently, many suppliers offer those discounts as a way to balance the equation with pure e-commerce retailers, who can then offset any investment they might make in a physical space with the savings they gain from discounts on the costs of their products.

There was also a question of their profit margin. They had two kinds of orders: small parcel orders and freight orders, with freight orders making up about 51 percent of their sales.

Because their order system didn't automatically give them the detailed information they needed, they put some effort into analyzing their orders to understand how much money they made on each type. It was then that they realized for the first time that they earned far more profit—about 15 percent more—on their small parcel orders than on freight sales.

They adjusted their marketing strategy to focus more on their small parcel products, while also looking for ways to reduce the shipping costs of all of their orders.

Then they tackled the rigors of forecasting by coming up with detailed, monthly cash-flow projections to see how the changes they made would affect their ability to make a profit while generating cash over the long term.

"We were so naive," Jesse told me. "It was amazing how much time and energy we were putting into traveling around and talking to investors rather than running our business. But when we switched our mind-set to work on growing slow and smart, we became profitable and retained ownership in our company. We're still learning, but it's hard to imagine where we would be today if we had brought on someone different as an investor. We feel like we're finally on our way."

It's unbelievable to see how much Jesse and Sam changed in just a year with the encouragement to stick to the basics of business. They have become empowered by learning to ask their suppliers and customers for help, something they didn't even know they could ask for. My hope is that their eyes have been opened and that they now have the tools and the scorecard to control their own destiny or to at least create the kind of business that gives them the balanced and happy life they want.

In a more recent phone call, Sam sounded upbeat and positive about where the business was headed. They had hired employees and were nearing completion of their brick-and-mortar store. Just as importantly, they had boosted their margins another 10 percent and got their cash flow under control. Perhaps most impressive to me was the fact that they nailed their forecast with 96 percent accuracy, which told me that they were listening to the right music.

Of course, there were still challenges to overcome. "Our biggest killer is the cost of freight," Sam told me. "Because we ship to different areas of the country, we have learned that not all the shippers are good at working with furniture, so we've also had to work around damages and returns from customers." The good news, however, was that he and Jesse still owned 100 percent of the business. They were working hard for the benefit of themselves and their children.

After sharing his updates with me, Sam told me he had to run. He was on his way to coach his kids' basketball team. That, I told him, was worth a million bucks all on its own.

I think the trap for so many entrepreneurs may be that they find themselves building a business rather than a life. They need to take both into consideration. To do that, they need to learn business and financial literacy skills to understand and evaluate the opportunities that present themselves.

I saw another example of what young entrepreneurs are being taught today when I was asked to invest in a technology start-up. The entrepreneur had developed what he thought was an exciting app that everyone would want. He, too, enrolled in an incubator where the coaches immediately pushed him to borrow as much money as he could from investors and banks—as well as his family and friends—so he could scale his app as quickly as possible. The instructors told him to swing big or go home. Well, that entrepreneur is still swinging, six years later, even though he now owes those investors and family members a total of $900,000. To his credit, he won't give up. He still thinks he can turn things around. But all that money has to feel like a monkey on his back. The worst part is that he is still asking for more money—a lot more—because he thinks that's what he needs to hit his business tipping point. Imagine that: a young guy in his early thirties, with a family, who already owes nearly $1 million—and he has no equity to show for it either! And this is what we are teaching young people these days about building a business.

Yet another story involves a young entrepreneur who used his family's life savings to buy a candle factory. He had graduated from a business program at a major university and thought he knew how businesses were run and operated. So rather than start a new business, he saw an opportunity to turn around an existing operation, something that would be far less risky. Unfortunately, what this entrepreneur learned after the deal closed was that the former owner had questionable financials. Rather than generating cash, the business was eating it for breakfast. Worse, the inventory numbers were all bogus, which meant the balance sheet was a fraud as well. Just a few years later, this young entrepreneur had no choice but to declare bankruptcy. As part of the deal, he now has to pay something like $1,200 a month for the next twenty years to pay off his debt, all while trying to support his young family.

While this guy was obviously a victim of a con job by the seller, it does beg the question of whether he really understood the basic rules of business before he made the deal. Did he have the savvy to pore over the financials, or to even walk through and take a hard look at the inventory? "We did do some due diligence on the financials and our attorneys did as well," he told me. "What we did not anticipate is that our willingness to trust would be taken advantage of. Quite a lesson."

My goal is not to blame the victim here but to point out that unless we teach our young entrepreneurs the basics of running a business—not simply advise them to borrow as much money as they can or grow as fast as they can—we'll be staring at even more tragedies like this in the years ahead.

I can't decide if I'm more sad or mad at the fact that I keep running into talented and energetic entrepreneurs who are just trying to fulfill the American dream but are becoming tragedies instead because they're using the wrong system to run their businesses.

The good news is that when young entrepreneurs do learn the basics of putting the system in place, amazing things can result.

CHAPTER FIVE
THE RIPPLE EFFECT

G reat things often start from humble beginnings. It's usually just a spark that can set a chain reaction in motion, and before you know it, that chain reaction has become something unstoppable. One seemingly small and insignificant event can change outcomes and results—as well as people's lives—in extraordinary ways that can be hard to imagine. You see this kind of outcome when you teach someone to be a businessperson. The chain reaction you set off when you do this can fuel widespread changes. It can transform people's lives. It's what we call the ripple effect.

One of those ripple effects is cutting across the heartland of America. As you exit the interstate, you find yourself on a rural road that cuts through fields—you might see a tractor raking the dirt or a combine harvesting crops—while stands of giant cottonwood trees stand guard along the creeks and irrigation ditches. As you drive farther, you reach your destination, a modernized barn, built of tin and stone. It's surrounded by a meadow and pockets of forest connected by a trail that skirts a pond. There's even a gentle waterfall next to what looks like a perfect place to snap a selfie. But no one's there now because a celebration is taking place inside the barn: a wedding. Flowers are everywhere and it looks as if there's plenty of food as well. The bride's white dress stands out among the crowd of smiling people. The venue seems to be the perfect place to get married. And the online reviews and social media posts prove it. Many newlyweds make the time to share their experiences, rating it with five stars and saying things such as "It is an absolutely beautiful venue with an absolutely amazing staff!" or "This is the place of your dreams!" This is even before they head off on their honeymoon, which they can actually afford since the wedding venue is priced so people don't have to blow their life savings when they rent it.

But there's a catch: the venue is booked two years in advance. "Better call now if you want to reserve a prime fall weekend," said Kristin, the thirtysomething, millennial entrepreneur who built the venue on her family's land, which had been a cattle ranch for generations. Even if you make the time to visit the facility, you'd better call ahead if you'd like Kristin to give you a tour of her place. While her business is thriving—sales are several hundred thousand dollars a year—she has one rule: she doesn't work weekends. She reserves that time for her husband and their four-year-old son. Imagine that. An entrepreneur who runs a business that operates mostly on weekends, when everyone wants to get married, doesn't need to be there. Rather, she has built a team of employees and contractors whom she has taught to run the business just as well as she could. Talk about finding work-life balance. But why would employees do such a thing? Isn't she taking advantage of them? Hardly. She teaches them the rules of running the business and keeping score of their progress. When they win, they get to share in the proceeds from every successful marriage union they help facilitate. Can you imagine the ripple effect if every business were run as this one is? It turns out that teaching just a single person the rules of the game can set off a chain reaction that can ultimately have an impact on dozens and dozens of lives.

Okay, we need to make a confession: we've known Kristin for years. In fact, she started her professional career as an intern at an SRC division while she was finishing her college degree in marketing. She then stayed on at SRC, taking different jobs in our various divisions for about ten years, all while learning how those businesses earned a profit and generated cash.

While she grew up in an entrepreneurial family, Kristin told us it was working for SRC and learning how to succeed in business that really taught her the power of business. "I definitely learned a lot from my family," she told us. "But I wasn't interested in business until I got outside of my family. One of the things that I absolutely love and am grateful for is that even though my job was always marketing, playing the Great Game of Business made me a business-minded marketer. I wasn't just a creative colors-and-fonts person."

Kristin told us that her aha moment of recognizing the transformative power of the playing the Great Game system came when she was twenty-five years old and working for our consulting and educational division. It happened on a freezing-cold February day when an ice storm was on its way, threatening a visitor-experience event that Kristin was responsible for organizing. (At these events, people interested in learning more about the Great Game fly into Springfield to see our Living Lab in action.) Kristin had to decide whether to cancel the event or not. "It hit me like a stupid stick that if we cancelled the event, I would have to work to make up the sales for the rest of the year," she told us. "That's when I truly got it."

Eventually, Kristin went to work for a healthcare technology company. Even though she was still only in her twenties, she was quickly promoted to an executive role because she understood what made the business tick. "They were blown away that I could communicate in business in a way that people ten years older than me couldn't," she told us. "It made me realize that so many of my peers just never had the opportunity to learn the language of business."

But Kristin's journey as an entrepreneur, and as a carrier of the ripple effect, was just getting started. While she was still working for the Great Game of Business, she reached out to a midwestern digital marketing company that she thought could modernize the healthcare company's website. That's when she met the two owners of the marketing company, Chris and Josh. She learned that the pair had bootstrapped their young company using their own money; they never even thought about bringing on investors. As she got to know Chris and Josh and their small team, Kristin was impressed that there was a real sense of camaraderie and teamwork among all their employees. They had a spirit of tackling things together, and the firm was growing by leaps and bounds.

What Kristin didn't immediately see, however, was that Chris and Josh might grow themselves out of business. Even though their accountant told them they were profitable, they were constantly on the brink of running out of cash, sometimes just a day away from not having enough cash to pay their bills or make payroll.

Kristin invited Chris and Josh to attend a seminar at SRC so they could learn more about the Game if they were all going to work together. It turned out to be a game-changing experience for the two entrepreneurs.

What really blew them away was the chance to take a tour of the SRC factory and to talk to the employee-owners working on the line.

Chris and Josh said they couldn't believe how engaged and knowledge-able everyone seemed, and how the company gave them the power to make decisions.

That was when Chris and Josh began to think they'd love to have that same kind of culture in their business. "Our belief in transparency for the benefit of our team made it an ideal fit for us," said Josh. "It felt like the honest and right way to run a company and a way to give people the opportunity to be their best selves."

Chris and Josh decided to dip their toes into playing the system in their company with guidance from Kristin. They began holding weekly huddles and teaching their employees about the financial health of the business and how it made its money. What they soon recognized was that playing the system with their team helped them develop new levels of discipline, particularly related to cash management.

"While I had some loose ideas about accounting from college and my other jobs, it took playing the Game to really understand the inverse relationship between cash and growth," said Josh. "The more we ran through our numbers, the more it dawned on us that—oh my goodness—cash was the thing we need to be most worried about to sustain the business."

That was definitely an issue whenever they decided to hire a new employee. By working the numbers, they realized it would take about sixty days or so before new employees understood the business well enough to start billing for their time. This meant Chris and Josh needed to think about where their business was going to see if they could afford to bring on new people.

At the same time, the team also began routinely measuring how many days of cash they had, which was often only a total of three or four days at the start.

"I think there's a romantic part about playing the Game," said

Josh. "But we learned it also means you need a different mentality about finding the numbers you need and building the systems to get at them. It can be a big pill to swallow."

But by teaching their employees financial literacy, which was a struggle at times for some of the creative staff, the team began to develop a sense of enablement and confidence about where their business was headed. Admittedly, they tracked the wrong numbers at times and they didn't always start their meetings on time or on the scheduled day. But they kept at it, and a transformation began to occur. "Our culture shifted away from focusing on growth because we learned that revenue growth without profit is simply more work," said Josh.

> **Our culture shifted away from focusing on growth because we learned that revenue growth without profit is simply more work.**

Kristin continued to serve as an unofficial coach and cheerleader for Chris and Josh even after she left SRC to work for that healthcare company. One day, they asked her to join the team full time as their head of marketing. They told us that Kristin, beyond her marketing skills, also brought her seemingly endless supply of energy as well as knowledge about how the team could better embrace the HIP and forecasting process, which, ultimately, had a dramatic impact on the company's fortunes.

"Kristin helped us embrace the discipline of the Game when it came to learning how to dig for, track, and forecast the numbers in our business that mattered most," said Josh, "and everyone quickly learned the stories that they told."

Chris and Josh agree that because of their forward forecasting, they were able to avert cash flow shortages and sales slumps that would have put them out of business. "In each scenario, we saw the missteps coming and were able, as a team, to devise solutions," said Chris. "As owners, these would have been nearly fatal in terms of stress without our Great Game practices. Instead, we had the tools of foresight and the team carried the burden and solved the challenges together."

"It wasn't just a game we played," said Josh, "it became a part of the company, a pillar upon which we grew. It became a selling point to new employees, a benchmark for our success, and a sounding board for resolving our failures. Our customers loved it as well."

For her part, Kristin told us that she credits the people at the marketing firm—specifically Chris and Josh—for teaching her the power of the customer and the need to build a business around customer needs.

While Chris, Josh, Kristin, and their team remained focused on growing their company, another life-changing opportunity presented itself. The office they had rented for their people had formerly been a cold storage facility, which meant it took a lot of heat to keep it warm during the winter. When Josh visited the remote office one day, he noticed that people were wearing scarves around their feet so that they didn't run up the heating bill. He realized then they needed to make a change. They approached one of their clients, a large midwestern advertising agency, about renting some desk space for some of their remote employees.

When Chris and Josh met with their client, the owner of the advertising company, he said he didn't want to rent them any desk space. Rather, he wanted to buy the entire company.

The advertising agency was struggling to expand into the world of digital ad-tech and saw acquiring Chris and Josh's company as a logical way to do that. What also blew the agency away was that this young business was not only profitable but also had a five-year plan and a SWOT analysis—strengths, weaknesses, opportunities, and threats—

focused on what the barriers might be to reaching company goals.

Before they would agree to sell the business, Chris and Josh checked with their people, including Kristin. The one condition that the employees insisted on as part of any sale was to be allowed to continue playing the Game, which the advertising agency agreed to and included in the purchase agreement. "That was a deal breaker," said Josh. "I think they agreed to it because, they figured, why rock the boat?"

As it turns out, the sale of the company set the stage for a new act for Chris, Josh, and Kristin.

As part of their sale agreement, both founders stayed on for a few years to help the acquisition go smoothly. But once they had fulfilled their obligations, they both decided to move on, especially because neither one wanted to uproot his family away from their hometown as so many of their childhood friends had done.

As the marketing company was being assimilated into the larger business, Kristin, now in her early thirties, was already plotting her next move. She saw the growing need for wedding venues, so she began talking to her father about the possibility of leveraging their family land for a new business. She hatched an idea based on her experience in helping plan her sister's wedding. Using her financial and business literacy skills, she came up with a plan to create a new kind of wedding venue aimed at couples on a budget, which she ultimately delivered on. By cutting out some of the middlemen—which most event venues rely on for their operations—Kristin recognized that she could run a more profitable operation while still charging reasonable prices. She also was able to apply the customer acquisition skills she had learned while working at the marketing business to target exactly the kind of customer her competitors were overlooking. That helped her venue to become the most booked wedding venue in her area.

And she did it all without taking on any debt.

Kristin enjoys another advantage: by limiting the number of hours she works *in* her business, she has more time to invest in working *on* her business, which is a common challenge for small business owners. In other words, she works more on her business than in it. She also continues to develop contingency plans by always thinking about what could go wrong. "I look back at my time at SRC for teaching me how to analyze and understand my market," Kristin told us. "I know my market intimately and better than anyone else." Kristin told me she hasn't raised her prices in two years. If the economy tanks next year, she said, she'd rather be booked. "It's all about playing the long game," she said.

Kristin told us she started to get nervous about her business's future, not just because of a potential future recession but also because a slew of new competitors had entered the wedding-venue market. "It's become a booming market for many reasons," she told me. "I still command a sweet spot where I cater to the do-it-yourself bride who has a smaller budget to work with. I have doubled down on my market niche. But when I begin to forecast out ten years or more, I realize I will eventually begin to lose market share."

Rather than throwing up her hands, Kristin said she put her skills at analyzing market needs to use yet again. In particular, she wanted to find a way to diversify her business and her income. What she realized was that the entire market for wedding services had become saturated, including wedding photography services. When she looked at what the best and most experienced photographers were doing—the real pros who faced competition from new competitors entering the market—she saw that many of them had begun to offer teaching and coaching services to other photographers. In other words, they had created an entirely new business based on leveraging their knowledge and experience. "It was interesting to me that the best photographers, the ones with a national reputation, had become educators," Kristin told us. "They had found a way to create a new revenue stream to supplement what they had begun to lose from shooting weddings." Kristin figured she could do the same.

She then created an online course for other wedding-venue owners. Over an eight-week period, she would teach them everything she knew about the business, including how to market to the perfect customer and how to get five-star reviews. She priced the course at $5,000 a pop, and before she knew it, she had fifteen venue owners from eleven different states sign up. "It was a completely scalable business model that includes group coaching where people are learning from each other," Kristin told us. "And I basically have no overhead." While she realized the number of potential customers for her business was finite, she also knew that just landing twelve customers a year would provide a healthy income of $60,000, with an allotment of just eight weeks of her time. She created a new business because she was focused on her contingency plans against potential adverse events.

For Kristin, however, her new business isn't just about the income. It's also about the impact she's now having on the lives of other would-be entrepreneurs, many of them women who have jumped into the wedding-venue business and struggled. Kristin told us about a mother-daughter team who had opened a venue and, after just a few months, were already burned out and ready to quit. "They told me it wasn't what they thought it would be," Kristin said. Another woman had struggled badly to book any events. Despite thirty inquiries and several tours of her facility, she didn't have a single reservation, which was making her think about quitting. But thanks to Kristin's help and training, all of these women have already turned their businesses around. "I just got an email from a woman who was struggling to book events before she took my class," Kristin told us. "And she recently booked four of the five people she gave tours to. That's like $20,000 of business for her. I'm so excited for her. She told me that rather than suffering through sleepless nights, now she has a strategy and a line of sight to find success."

This is what we mean by the ripple effect. You take one person, teach her the rules of business, and watch her take off. Only now, she is having an impact on other people by teaching them what she knows. "I am so grateful for all of the experiences I have had in business along the way," Kristin told us. "I am so proud to be able to pay it forward and use that knowledge to help others. I'm not the smartest person in the world. But I do know business, which all started with learning to play the system. It really set me up to become a successful small business owner, and to teach others to do the same."

And the chain reaction that began when Kristin joined us at SRC as an intern didn't stop there. The impact she had on Chris and Josh has rippled forward as well.

REBOOTING A BUSINESS

After they sold their business and moved on, Chris and Josh decided they wanted to go into business together again. And this time, they partnered up with Drake, a young entrepreneur Chris mentored. For his part, Drake had worked with his brother and sister-in-law in running a home gardening and landscaping business. It was small but successful. Until he met Chris, Drake had never heard about the Great Game of Business. But the more Drake learned about it and put the system into place in his business, the more he began to appreciate that his gardening business would never be able to scale beyond just serving a few homes at a time. Armed with this new knowledge, he was eager to join Chris and Josh in their next venture, a place where they might be able to grow something with the help of playing the Great Game.

While the three partners wanted to do something new together, they also decided they wanted to run a business that involved something very different from web development. They began working with a business broker, who floated an opportunity that was just about the polar opposite of selling online marketing services. The business sold industrial refrigeration parts to breweries and meat processing plants. A sole proprietor ran it, with part-time help from his wife and daughter. At first, the trio passed up the opportunity because there was nothing sexy about refrigeration.

But when they took a look at the numbers for the business, using the skills they had developed by playing the system, things began to take on a whole new light. They saw that the business could quickly generate positive cash flow and that, by using their digital marketing skills, they could also modernize its sales and marketing system.

They decided to pull the trigger and buy the business and, from the first day they owned it, they began playing the system with their seven employees. "This time around we were able to design the Game the way we wanted to without having to rewind or reset expectations," said Chris. "It just felt right from the start." The new business includes an entire room full of scoreboards tracking the financials as well as five-year forecasts.

"We learned that if you want to make good decisions and empower your people, you need scoreboards for them to understand that you are going somewhere together," said Josh. "I don't know how you'd run a business without them." The Monday morning huddles, in which the whole team walks through their scoreboards while eating breakfast together, have become a highlight of the week.

Just as important, Chris, Josh, and Drake learned that understanding the financials and the critical importance of cash flow brought them the freedom of having their business work for them and not the other way around.

"When I talk to friends my age who work for companies that aren't open book, it's sad to see how much they hate going to work," Drake told us. "I feel I want to give them a job so they can learn what it means to be free and how they can affect their own future." They had found a sense of freedom by sharing the stress. These guys got it.

CHAPTER SIX
FREE MARKETS; FREE PEOPLE

The transformative power of business is not exclusive to America; it's universal. I saw this firsthand when I was honored to serve as the American judge on a panel charged with choosing an Entrepreneur of the World, an award sponsored by a major consulting company. While I had judged similar Entrepreneur of the Year awards back in the United States, this time I was invited to fly to Monte Carlo for the globally focused event.

It was odd timing in that I was feeling pretty low about the prospects for the world at that time. Stories about war, poverty, and famine dominated the headlines on a daily basis. I was desperate for a spark of hope.

As I began reading through the case studies of the finalists in the contest, which represented companies from thirty-seven countries, my mood began to brighten. Their businesses aimed at turning their countries around, using democracy rather than bureaucracy and state ownership. Rather than waiting for the government to deliver a top-down solution to their problems, these entrepreneurs turned to commerce for bottom-up answers. They created free markets to help free their people.

One story that really stood out to me concerned an Eastern European candidate who had started an underground printing press as a way to fight against the oppressive martial-law government that ruled his country at the time. He would print up to eighty thousand leaflets on repressive social issues, which he and his friends would distribute in an effort to bring about constructive democratic changes, often putting their own lives at risk. Over time, that printed material helped create a movement that contributed to bringing freedom and democracy not only to that country but across Eastern Europe as well. What's remarkable is that the entrepreneur behind that movement continued to build his printing operation into one of the largest companies of its kind in Europe. It really blew me away to read about someone who had used the media to bring people together and create positive changes, which is not what the media is doing these days. This guy was a true entrepreneurial hero who gave back to his community and country.

As I read about similar stories happening across the world, my batteries began to recharge. It was incredibly inspiring to see how the freedom to exercise choice can result in security and stability across the globe.

If I could nominate a candidate for that award today, it might be Dave, an entrepreneur in Canada. Dave grew up working in the business his parents started in the 1970s, a commercial supplier of trees and plants to retailers in the United States and Canada, but he never intended to run it.

"I didn't want to do what my dad did," he told me. But when his dad offered him a job after he finished college in 1995, Dave couldn't say no. "I wasn't in love with growing plants, but I loved the idea of growing and shaping a business," he said. He eventually took over as president of the business in 2007, and in 2012, he bought out his parents and sister to become the firm's sole owner.

Dave is one of those entrepreneurs who are always hunting for the answers to the challenges facing their business. He considers himself a "dedicated learner." As a result, he has experimented with just about any and every business management fad that has come along. That constant hunt eventually led him to the Great Game system. While it might not have been clear to him at the start, the system was just what he needed to address the thorniest obstacles standing in the way of his business's growth, starting with himself. He simply couldn't make every decision fast enough. He became the constraint to the company's ability to grow. "I finally realized that I couldn't come up with all the ideas on my own." Dave wanted every one of his team members to think and act as an owner of the business. "I didn't want to make all the decisions. I wanted more freedom."

One of the key hurdles Dave needed to overcome with the help of his people is the seasonal nature of his business: some 80 percent of all shipments occur during just four weeks in the spring. That places enormous pressure on the nursery to get the right mix of products ready at the right time. It's controlled chaos during prime growing season as dozens of trucks stream constantly in and out of the gates leading to the farm's four different locations, all of which need to be loaded by hand with the correct orders. Every plant counts. Margins are tight and the weather can have a dramatic effect on the season.

As a result, Dave leans heavily on his team of more than one hundred associates to help during the planning and organization as the prime growing season arrives. "I don't want to be a one-man band," he told me. "I want to build a company that will outlast me."

But that leads to the other significant challenge Dave faces in his business: building a cohesive culture that brings together his team, most of whom are immigrants or political refugees from thirteen different countries such as Mexico, Iraq, Sudan, Zimbabwe, China, Costa Rica, Ecuador, Chile, Brazil, Argentina, Peru, and India.

"The majority of our team speaks English as a second language, so communication is often difficult," Dave told me. "People's education levels also vary, where some people are illiterate while we have a few people who have master's degrees from other countries."

Not only are those language barriers difficult to manage, but there are cultural differences as well, which has an impact on how people communicate with each other—or not. "We are blessed with a very dedicated and talented staff," Dave said. "I work very hard to make sure our company culture is such that we are able to attract and retain people well. While there are odd exceptions, we have had very few, less than five, people quit our place in many, many years."

Part of the reason for that impressive retention rate was the company's transparent culture. Dave told me that he and his family had always embraced a deep belief in sharing information with their associates and finding ways to help them overcome hurdles in their jobs.

"My parents have always had a philosophy of learning, growing, taking a chance, having fun, and keeping the big picture of life in mind," Dave told me. "From that mind-set, we have always believed in treating our staff well. For example, they started our ongoing tradition of making lunch for all staff once a month and having a meeting where we shared many things, including revenue, customer stories, problems, and challenges. Everything except profit."

But when he held all-company quarterly meetings to share the company's goals with the team, he struggled to get past the language and cultural barriers that kept everyone from working from the same page. "I knew there was something missing whenever we had a staff meeting," Dave said. "I felt a desire to do more with our people, but I didn't know how to do this. I even had a large mural painted on our ceiling, which said, 'Everyone an Entrepreneur.' But there was still a disconnect."

Then Dave found hope and a new way of looking at things through the Great Game system.

The more he learned, the more convinced he became that the system could help him transform the culture of his organization in a way that also helped his associates grow as the business grew. "My worldview and my experiences led me to conclude that trusting people to run the company was much better than me trying to do it myself," Dave told me. "I wanted to build something that would last, and build something into the lives of our people, as well as make a statement to the world about my beliefs around capitalism and culture."

The system has brought the company together in a common culture and is helping to create a common language. "It reduces barriers when people are working toward the same goal," Dave told me. "It also turns out that other people can make better decisions and generate better ideas anyway. If my associates can come up with them, they will own those ideas and run with them. I truly want them to think of our company as their company. I want to earn their heads, their hands, and their hearts. I truly believe that culture eats strategy for breakfast."

All of the associates now attend a daily huddle, as well as weekly forecasting meetings, which are conducted in English, Spanish, and sometimes Punjabi. To help everyone keep up to speed, scoreboards have also been put up at the four different farm sites the nursery operates—all of which has helped drive significant cost savings throughout the company.

"The difference that Great Game system has made is that it brings everyone into the full picture," Dave told me. "To create lasting cultural change, we are relentless in our meeting rhythms. Our over-arching goal is to use the system's tools and mind-set to develop our people and grow the company. We have to be very intentional in our education programs because many of our associates are shy about asking questions in a big group. We try to break out into smaller groups, so they get a chance to speak up. The result is that everyone knows what we are making, and most have an idea of what can be done to improve the financial picture."

The most important thing any leader can do is teach all their team members what game they're in. When you do that, people begin to look at the business from a different perspective. It becomes something more than work and reminds me of the story of the three masons: A man is walking along a road and comes upon three masons. The man asks each of the masons, "What are you doing?" The first mason replies, "I am laying bricks." The second mason says, "I'm building a wall." The third mason says, "I am building a cathedral." Wouldn't you like to have everyone working with you thinking big like that?

As a result of his associates looking at their roles differently, Dave said the company saw some early big wins in areas such as cutting better deals with suppliers. He also changed his sales team's compen-sation system. They had been paid a commission on top-line growth even if a deal they closed didn't generate any profits for the business. Now, commissions are gone, and they participate in the profit share program. "Our sales guys used to operate as individuals," said Dave. "Now they work like a team."

Dave has now set his sights on getting more of his associates who work on the front lines to go further in their financial literacy training, moving beyond the income statement and into the cash flow statement and balance sheet. He also wants to get everyone more involved in setting the strategic direction of the business by getting them to participate in the company's HIP process. Dave's particularly interested in generating ideas about how the nursery can diversify and begin to generate revenue beyond its peak season in the spring. Ideas currently on the table include everything from aquaponics to licensing their sophisticated in-house inventory and ordering software for other nurseries to purchase and use.

Dave might be most proud of the Game's help in expanding the horizons of those associates who come from different countries. He pointed to the fact that some of his associates from Mexico worked for six to eight months and then, in the off-season each year, returned to their homes, where life can be difficult. Many of them, Dave said, don't have running water in their homes or even more than dirt for a floor. These workers used money they saved from their paychecks and bonuses to start their own business, buy land to grow crops such as potatoes or avocados, or simply send their kids to a better school. Dave remembered a day when he went to say goodbye to a man named Rolando. "I said, 'See you next year,'" said Dave. "But Rolando told me he wasn't coming back. He told me, 'I used the business education I got here to start my own business.' He said he had bought some land for a farm and started an internet café. He also bought a car to start a taxi business. It gave me such hope that we were making a big impact on other people's lives. Playing the Game has been a very rewarding journey for me. The more we've shared, the more we have received in return. My goal is to preach capitalism and Christianity; free markets and free people. I know if I can be successful, I can make a difference in someone's life. I wish more leaders had the nerve and a bigger vision to play the Game and have that same kind of wide-ranging impact as well."

CHAPTER SEVEN
UNLEASHING THE CREATIVES

A while back, my wife, Betsy, served on the board of a local community theater, something she got involved in because our youngest daughter was interested in pursuing a career in the arts. The theater, which is more than one hundred years old, attracted something like two hundred volunteers who helped support the dozen or so folks who worked there full time. At the time Betsy joined the board, the theater had just hired a new director from New York. He had been brought in with the idea that he could direct and promote the cutting-edge plays he had been known for in his work on Broadway. Everyone was excited that this director would bring different kinds of performances to the Midwest, unlike anything the theater had presented in its long history.

Whenever she got back from one of the board meetings, Betsy would tell me that they had endless conversations about the plays, the costumes, and the set designs. The director promised that everything was going to be "state of the art." The board discussed every aspect of the theater, everything except the budgets and the financials, which usually got mentioned only in passing at the end of every meeting. That got Betsy concerned. She began asking me to come with her to a meeting so I could take a look at the copies of the theater's financial reports. I always found an excuse to say no. I didn't think I could add anything to the arts. Then, one December, after she begged me once again to come to a meeting, I agreed to go—but only as an observer.

As everyone took their seats in rickety folding chairs, the conversation immediately turned to various aspects of the latest productions. They talked about everything they needed to do in the upcoming season. I felt totally out of my element and began to ask myself why I was there. I'm not sure I have ever been as uncomfortable as I was in that creaky metal chair. I was definitely going to let Betsy know that she owed me one for this. Finally, as they concluded the discussion of the seasonal program for the next year, someone casually mentioned that they didn't have enough money to make payroll for the full-time employees that month.

I just about fell out of my chair when I heard this. It was as if a bomb had gone off inside my head. This was a crisis situation. And yet they hadn't spent more than five minutes talking about money, budgets, financials, and payrolls. I sat there wondering how they could not make payroll and it was two weeks until Christmas! I sat there, gripping the edge of my seat, my knuckles turning white, waiting for someone, anyone, to say something. Nobody did.

So I stood up and asked, "How can we not make payroll?" Quite frankly, I was angry and had lost most of my patience by that point. We had never missed a payroll in more than forty years in our business. The only thing I could think about was all the kids who might not get Christmas presents. And still nobody said anything. I was furious. Rather than wait any longer for an answer, I wrote out a check to cover what they needed. Betsy and I then headed home, taking with us the theater's books and a twelve-pack of beer I picked up on the way.

We stayed up the whole night with the books spread out on the kitchen table trying to figure out what had been going wrong, while also looking for a path to make this thing successful. I also looked at the theater's organizational chart and noticed that there was no name in the box for a sales and marketing person. I asked Betsy why the theater hadn't hired anyone for that role. She told me that it was because the director thought it was more important to hire a set designer. A set designer, when they couldn't make payroll? I couldn't believe it. I was out of my mind. There were only so many checks I was willing to write.

As we continued to work through the numbers, the story of why the theater was struggling became clear. The theater had a capacity of 650 seats but was only drawing an average crowd of 250 per performance. Worse, several of the patrons—companies and organizations that ran cosponsorship programs with the theater—had backed away from their financial commitments because of the line-up. Even the volunteer support seemed to be waning. It seemed clear to me that the theater wasn't putting on plays people wanted to come and see. While the new director wanted to continue to create artsy productions, he didn't seem to consider whether anyone actually wanted to see them. And by doing that, he put the theater, and the jobs of the people who worked there, at risk of failure. They didn't need a new set designer; they needed a sales and marketing person who could drum up community interest in their performances. That was the transformation they needed: to make the shift from just creating individual plays to thinking of the theater as their major responsibility.

It was obvious that the theater's critical number—the one thing that could sink it—was ensuring a butt sat in every available seat. They needed to start thinking about what their customers were willing to buy tickets to. Now that can be a hard adjustment for some creative people such as that theater's director. In his mind, just making his art was enough. But what if he began to use his creative powers to engineer new products and to tap new markets that would then allow his theater to flourish in a sustainable way? It was critical to get all the staff members to understand that they needed to think beyond their individual responsibilities and look at their theater in a new, bigger light. They needed to understand that they could all make a difference—if they were all working on the same goal.

While addressing that critical number of butts in seats was crucial to getting things back on track, we also needed to tackle a bigger issue: getting everyone involved in the theater to think and act as if they were owners. When I think about what ownership means, I think about empowerment, freedom, trust, clear roles, and goals. That's what I call psychic ownership. I think about people's ability to make a difference, to understand what they can do, and how to apply themselves to do it. In my experience, anyone can begin to feel and act as an owner would, whether they own equity or not. We're talking about achieving a different mind-set. We want people to try to take responsibility for their jobs, to have a sense of pride in what they do, and to feel they're making a difference to each other as a result.

What we're really trying to do is get as many people as possible working toward a shared, mutually beneficial goal from which everyone benefits. Ownership is that fire in the belly, that motivation to tackle a task not just for yourself, but also for the people around you. You might have psychic ownership of a line on the cash flow statement such as ticket sales, or a production expense on the income statement such as costumes, and you treat that money as if it were your own. And when something has been done well to help make the entire organization successful, you want to raise your fist in the air and celebrate.

We look at ownership as teamwork. It's not just about working a job for eight hours and then going home. It's about developing a real sense of commitment and involvement, knowing that if you don't follow through on your responsibilities, you let someone else down. You begin to think outside yourself. You need to feel that sense of responsibility and commitment to whatever you are embarking upon. You are responsible for the plan and the results because you made the plan. You own the task and the outcome. It all comes back to making a commitment to do well, not just for you but also for others.

When you feel you are an owner, you become stronger, more competitive, and you begin to differentiate yourself in the market-place. I see ownership as engagement, the tool that allows people to truly respect the contributions from each and every person in the organization.

We wanted to change their mind-set. We wanted these incredibly creative artists to start thinking that the theater, their business, was their real product, not just the plays they were putting on stage. It wasn't enough that the employees were working hard on their individual tasks; we needed to get them thinking about the big picture: what it was going to take to make the theater financially viable. The incentive was clear that unless big changes were made, the theater, and their jobs, would be lost.

The first big change happened when the director from New York quit (you could also say he was encouraged to leave). As soon as he realized that he was going to be accountable for his decisions, he probably figured he was in way over his head. It was a great example of addition by subtraction.

We then decided to create an incentive program for the employees, based on audience attendance at the performances. We charged them with finding new ways to get people into the seats to improve the theater's cash flow. One great example of their teamwork in action was when they realized on their own that they needed to perform plays that had a much wider appeal than the ones they had previously been staging. They recognized that they needed to start performing plays that involved kids, which would then draw in parents and grandparents, maybe even neighbors too, all of whom would buy tickets and pack the place. Once the team started to see results, they stuck with the program and continued to come up with better ideas. After about four months, they were generating enough cash flow to cover not only the payroll but also some needed maintenance on the theater. They were on their way to making their bonus.

We were also fortunate to promote one of the theater's star performers, a woman named Beth, to take over as artistic director. Unlike the director she replaced, Beth bought into the system right from the start even though she had always avoided math like the plague, dating back to her grade school algebra class. But she was willing to take on new challenges, given the stakes at risk. "In my first year all of us were motivated to keep our jobs," Beth told me. "We knew we all had to develop an accountability to the numbers, to be willing to change. We had to run pretty lean and mean. We also had to keep people informed about what we were doing and why we were doing it. It used to be easy to think that anything having to do with the numbers didn't affect me. That all changed. We realized that without the open communication the system brought us, we could end up in hell."

Beth and her team made use of anything they had on hand, such as used desk calendars, which they then hung on their walls as score-boards to track their progress on their goals. "Creative people are such visual creatures," she told me. "I personally love those thermometers that fill up the closer you get to your goals. We all found it so exciting to track our progress together. It gave us accountability to each other, and it helped bring us even closer together as a team."

One day, Beth called me to discuss an idea she had. Beth and her team had decided that they wanted to put together a production of *Beauty and the Beast*. But to do that, she figured they needed about $20,000 to create the high-end costumes that would really blow the audience away. What she didn't know was where she could get that kind of money. She started by creating a business plan.

Beth's idea was the theater could tap into a new entrepreneurial fund that had been set up by United Way and allowed nonprofits to access low-interest loans to build new programs. She could borrow the money she needed for the costumes, but she didn't stop there. After some searching online, Beth and her team found that something like twenty other theaters across the country were also planning a produc-tion of the show. In her business plan, she speculated that the theater could rent their costumes to other theaters, something she figured could be worth $7,500 a show. Even if she just rented the costumes four times, she could bring in another $30,000 annually. I thought it was a brilliant idea.

After our conversation, Beth and her team put the plan into action, and it raised about $60,000 in just six months. She blew her plan away. That was a breakthrough moment for the theater, and it helped pay off, eighteen months early, the loan taken out to make the costumes. "That was the foundation for us to diversify our stream of income," Beth told me, "and we have continued to build on that foundation. I now find it exciting to tackle challenges and find ways to squeeze $20 out of every $1 we spend." Once Beth understood the system and the power of diversification, she transformed as a person. It was her aha moment. She was no longer just an actor, producer, or director; she had become a businessperson. Once that kind of mind shift happens, it changes your life forever.

To this day, any time they perform a play, Beth and her team are thinking about how to produce revenue beyond the play itself. More recently, they created a new stream of income by renting out the stage sets they have designed and built. "There's often a problem with the mind-set in nonprofits that don't have to make money," Beth told me. "I've learned to look at this like a business, where you don't just zero out your books at the end of the year. We always need to be creative in finding ways to fund ourselves so we can control our own destiny. If you're not growing, you're dying."

One year, Beth and her team decided to stage a production of the play *The Full Monty*, which, if you're unfamiliar with it, features a cast of male strippers. I thought they had perhaps pushed the envelope too far with that choice. But it was a smash hit and people loved it, which didn't come as a surprise to Beth and her team. They had begun to understand what their customers wanted and when they could put on a more edgy production or something the other theaters, their competition, might shy away from. The team also learned to appreciate the power of having contingency and backup plans to help ensure they could recover if a performance didn't measure up to expectations. "I have learned it's about getting ahead of stuff and embracing open communication," Beth told me. "We have learned to follow through on answering the question of What if? As long as the right hand knows what the left hand is doing, life is good. Otherwise, you have the head asking why."

Beth and her team are already working on their next project

to help put them ahead of their competition: They are running a campaign to raise several million dollars in capital to purchase another theater in town. That theater is about one-third the size of their existing theater—it has about 185 seats—which will give them the ability to stage performances that don't have to appeal to as large an audience. Beth said this was important because, in analyzing the trends in the market and seeing what her competition was offering, she and her team recognized that making room for nonmusical plays or comedy acts was important to their customer base. "As we take the temperature of what the community is looking for, we see the need to continue to diversify the kind of performance we can offer," she told me. It's easier to invent in an organization such as this one when you know your investments are going to get results.

The challenge with creative people can be making sure you give them the tools they need to avoid running out of cash, because once you get them turned on with all their gifts, talents, and amazing ideas—Holy Christmas!—they take off like rocket ships. When you can see the moment the light bulb goes on inside people's eyes—snap!—it's a wonderful thing to see people realize that once they do something for the first time, they can do it again, and again, and again. It becomes a pattern of thought.

As a testament to their success, Beth and her team have grown their annual budget over a fifteen-year period from a starting point of $450,000 up to about $2 million today. Another big driver of that growth has been the expansion of yet another diversified income stream developed by the theater: an education program designed to give young people the opportunity to perform in the community while also teaching them the skills they might need to one day turn their passion into a career. That program is run by Lorianne, another theater employee, who also happens to be an extremely accomplished ballerina and a nationally recognized choreographer. "The education program is aimed at people looking for that preprofessional training ground," Lorianne told me. "We can now boast of having one of the elite programs in the country that helps people gain employment in the arts." And it's not just the performing arts. The program recently launched a new film laboratory to train young people to produce videos. Lorianne believes they can generate income from the lab by giving kids the experience of making marketing videos for local businesses that might not have the budgets to hire big advertising firms. Part of the reason behind purchasing the new building is to provide more room for the education program and the number of students it can serve. Doesn't it make you wonder why we aren't offering similar kinds of education to *all* of our kids?

Lorianne admits that she and her team are always bursting with new ideas about how they can expand their program, but the system serves as a guidepost to evaluate which of those initiatives are the ones they should really pursue. They also include their volunteers and their students in huddles as a way to keep them connected to what they are doing, and why they are doing it.

"Going back to the numbers helps you distill those ideas into what is actually going to propel the bottom line forward," she told me. "The sky is the limit—as long as you can pay for it. We use a checklist to ask ourselves, during our weekly huddle, How do we serve the bottom line? Just like we serve our students, our staff, and the community, we have to treat the bottom line equally. It's also getting people to understand that every single person can make a difference and that even minor changes in our budget can have major impacts on the bottom line."

By learning to better evaluate where to invest their time and money, Lorianne has been able to not only expand the number of kids she can have an impact on but create a thriving business as well. When the program launched, it generated $20,000 in income with a couple dozen kids participating. Things have only exploded from there, as income from the program is now almost $600,000 a year, touching the lives of more than one thousand kids a year. "We are helping people build their dreams," Lorianne told me. "And the you-gotta-wanna is the strongest part to building a way of life." Perhaps just as exciting, Lorianne said that several of the graduates of the education program have gone on to start their own businesses in the arts—and they've taken the lessons of the Game with them.

Lorianne told us that some degree of business education is needed for some of her students when they first enroll in the program, and it is also needed for any new members they add to their staff. "Many of them have stars in their eyes when they come to work here," she said. "They think it's all about dancing around and being clever. But then the sirens start to go off when they begin to realize the intensity of the work. There's a learning curve for them to appreciate that it's called 'show business' and not 'show arts.' We have to teach them that profit isn't a dirty word. Profit isn't such a bad thing when you're talking about having a quality of life where the staff can be paid living wages. That's not happening in every arts organization. I've been told that 97 percent of people who want to be actors are unemployed. For those of us who get to enjoy full-time jobs working in the arts, profit is a wonderful thing."

> **For those of us who get to enjoy full-time jobs working in the arts, profit is a wonderful thing.**

An important lesson that fine arts colleges and public universities could learn is the value of teaching creative people about business. Lorianne told me that most people interested in the arts leave the field by the time they're thirty-five years old because they don't make any money. What about those who study piano? Might they want to run a piano company some day? It still seems that the artistic mind-set is to hope and pray for a benefactor, an entitlement attitude on the lines of if you build it, they will come. But they don't always come. It's like hoping you will win the lottery some day without buying a ticket.

Beth, Lorianne, and their team remain artists at heart. But once they got the idea of ownership, they began to think differently. One of the things we often hear business owners say is, "If only I could get my employees to think like owners." They're looking for that you-gotta-wanna spirit, that burning desire to go the extra mile. One way to do it is to give them their own shares in the company. But that's not always practical—and I also don't think it's essential. There is something more powerful that goes beyond a stock certificate. What you can do, regardless of the kind of organization you work in, is develop a mind-set of psychic ownership—that inner pride and sense of self-esteem—that can truly unleash the creative power of your people. That's the sweet spot where people truly begin to feel they can grab the brass ring for themselves. As Beth and Lorianne told me: "If everyone would embrace playing the Game, the entire world would change. We know the system changes lives because it's changed ours."

CHAPTER EIGHT

YOU CAN'T HAVE VALUES WITHOUT PERFORMANCE

The millions of people around the country who work for so-called nonprofit organizations are heroes and heroines. These are folks who are drawn to a noble cause, a purpose bigger than themselves, in sectors such as education, healthcare, and community building. We admire each and every one of them for the size of their heart and for being motivated to make the world a better place.

Unfortunately, it's some of these same folks who tend to see for-profit organizations as greedy and self-serving. The idea that non-profits would make a profit—a four-letter word if there ever were one—from their efforts is unthinkable.

There's a sizable gap people need to bridge to become aware that a nonprofit can learn from a for-profit organization. Sure, it makes sense for nonprofits to invite business owners and leaders to join their board because they need funding resources. They might ask business leaders to review and approve their annual budget, but they're not really looking for significant input. That's where the connection stops. Help in the form of donations and volunteers, not insights from businesspeople are what nonprofits seek. Nonprofits and for-profits represent completely opposing sets of values, right?

It's our position that whether you run a nonprofit or a for-profit organization you still get the same report card: your financials. You can sugarcoat the terminology all you want. We realize that most of these folks went to school to become public servants, not to learn about revenue and earnings. But to run a nonprofit, you still have to manage cash and bring in enough revenue—excuse me, donations—to pay your people and cover your costs so they can go out and do some good in the world.

The tension here is that if nonprofits don't understand how to manage their financial performance, they can't deliver on the values to their communities—no money, no mission. That can be a delicate message to sell to people who often see business as the enemy.

The paradox is that the Game is an ideal fit with the passionate people who work for nonprofits. It can help them to learn that the better they manage their financial performance, the more good they can do in the world. It's an incredibly powerful recipe when you start with people who already have an electric passion for what they do—to serve a higher calling—and then teach them the system.

It's a message that a woman named Katie has taken to heart. Katie was promoted to the position of CEO of a well-known nonprofit when she was just twenty-seven years old. The nonprofit was part of a national organization that had some three hundred agencies nationwide, all of which had the mission of supporting children, especially those from single-parent homes. While she was honored to be tapped into the role by the previous executive director and board president, the idea that she was qualified for the role was, as she put it to me, "an outright lie." She did have a master's degree in nonprofit management, but she had only been working in the nonprofit world for three years when she was promoted to lead this organization. When she and all of the other executive directors gathered at their national conference, Katie quickly realized that she was the youngest in the room—by a lot.

"I think the one advantage I had in being so young was that I was willing to admit that I didn't have all the answers and that I needed to rely on the knowledge and experience from the rest of the staff in order to succeed," Katie told me.

Katie was also willing to listen and lean on her board for help, especially after one board member introduced her to the idea of playing the Game. He worked at a company that played the Game, and he did his best to sell her on the idea that she could empower her staff by sharing the agency's financials with them and teaching them how they could improve their performance. He also encouraged her to think about how she could give her team a stake in the outcome when they exceeded their goals. Since there was no equity to hand out, he thought she should consider paying a bonus.

Katie just about had a heart attack when she heard that. Pay a bonus? In a nonprofit? She wasn't even sure if that was ethical; it might even be illegal.

"It was a very controversial idea," Katie told me. "I had been warned about not paying out commissions or bonuses based purely on profit. The IRS had a twelve-factor test of compensation, and I assumed that a stake in the outcome would violate that test. The key piece that my board helped me to see was that the stake in the outcome had to be tied to performance in terms of program growth and financial growth. This is why we ended up calling it a growth incentive instead of a bonus. It was simply our incentive for growing the mission of the organization if we had the financial means to do so."

But there were also psychological barriers for her staff and other board members to overcome, particularly guilt. After all, it was the Puritans who helped redefine the modern concept of charity, which was a way for them to repent their sins by giving away money. Working for a cause should be seen as a sacrifice, not a way to earn a living.

"There is a myth in the nonprofit world where people think that the best charities are the ones where 99 percent of the revenue goes to the mission," Katie told me. "I began to challenge people by asking if they'd rather have $100 in revenue where $99 goes to the mission, or $1 million in revenue where $750,000 went to the program? I would make the argument that we could do more good if we could scale. But to do that sustainably, we needed to invest more in our people."

One way Katie's team could do that was through a variable compensation program such as a growth incentive. Despite the criticism from the naysayers, it's a more responsible way to reward the staff for their performance than a fixed compensation program is. It also protects the organization's mission when times get tough or they hit a black swan.

The idea of rewarding the staff financially for efforts to increase donations or reduce costs was also important in terms of helping reduce staff turnover, which is a constant plague in most nonprofits. Katie said that it was typical for employees to accept a position in the nonprofit sector for less money than they were making in the for-profit sector because they were passionate about the mission, but that passion can quickly fade away in tough times, leading to burnout and staff leaving for higher-paying jobs.

But agencies like hers weren't really counting the true costs of that turnover to their organization, which can sometimes be 1.5 times someone's salary.

"I began to understand that staff retention was important," said Katie, "and that they deserved to be compensated and rewarded for their hard work."

Katie's board member encouraged her to think about how playing the Game might help her better engage her team in delivering their mission and pay them better at the same time.

She agreed to start slowly, first by holding huddles and explaining the financials to the team. "I believe that my lack of experience made me open to playing the Game," Katie told me. "Being so young also gave me the humility I believe every player needs to start playing."

The same year she started as executive director, the organization was also getting a new agency information management (AIM) system. The AIM system allowed Katie and her team to input all of their program metrics into one centralized database so they could measure their impact nationwide. It also allowed them to benchmark against other organizations to see who had the best metrics and in what areas.

"Before AIM, we thought we were measuring our programs' success just fine through a spreadsheet," Katie told me. "But it wasn't until the initial report was finalized that reality set in. Our numbers didn't look good. In fact, in some areas we were in the bottom 10 percent compared to our peers. This was a major blow to the morale within the agency, especially to our case managers. They were working so hard every day for very little pay because they believed in the mission. To see that their work wasn't making as big an impact as they had thought was very disheartening."

Then, things got worse.

Katie made a trip to the state capitol to attend a meeting with the five other agencies that operated in her state. "We assembled once a year to talk about our lobbying efforts and future opportunities for funding as a state coalition," Katie told me. What made this meeting different was that the other organizations now had access to Katie's numbers via the AIM. That's when she got a reality check from the executive director of the largest agency in the state. "She said, 'Your numbers are bringing down the entire state and putting our funding at risk,'" Katie said. "She asked me, 'Do you have a plan to get these retention rates up?' All I could do was smile in return. I knew we were in trouble and needed to do something different once I got back home."

The following Monday after she got back to the office, Katie called a meeting with her staff. She had a tough message to deliver. "I told them it was no longer good enough just to do the best we can," Katie told me. "I told them there were other agencies across the state, even across the country, that were providing the exact same services and getting much better results. We needed to learn from them, we needed to track our progress, and we needed to get better. And we needed to get better not just to increase our funding or to be recognized for our work, but because we owed it to the kids in our community."

Katie thought the team could improve by embracing the Game at an even deeper level.

Nonprofits by their very nature have to be transparent with their financials. The difference is that they do open-book reporting without taking the extra step of embracing open-book management. "Our staff was always very numbers oriented," said Katie. "But they didn't understand how they could affect them. I was creating these financial reports for the board, but no one on staff was looking at them or asking questions about them."

The same thing was happening with the monthly reports the team received from the national agency: no one was thinking about what those numbers meant or how they could affect them. That dynamic changed when Katie and her team started setting goals and giving people ownership of them.

The staff of fourteen people was small enough for Katie to assign all staff members their own line item on the scoreboard. Over time, as they kept huddling, she slowly began to see the transformation. Her colleagues began to believe they could have an impact on the numbers even if they didn't have a math degree. "The scoreboard puts it out there, and the huddles give everyone a chance to talk about it," said Katie. "I have seen staff members who have hidden their entire lives from numbers finally step up in a huddle."

Katie remembers one caseworker with the agency who told her that she had studied social work specifically because she didn't want to have to deal with numbers. Katie encouraged the caseworker to adopt a different mind-set. "I asked her to think about the numbers not as a formula but as a story about why the number changed," Katie told me.

In time, that doubter became a true believer, someone who turned the corner and became a leader in the organization. "She became the biggest advocate of playing the Game," said Katie. "She would tell everyone that if she could do it, so could anyone."

Another issue Katie and her team faced concerned the agency team's division between the people who worked on raising donations (development), and the folks who worked with the kids and volunteers (programming). "We spent a lot of time getting everyone on the same page," said Katie. "We had people in programming saying development needed to work harder raising money and then we had people in development saying the program people needed to do more. The system helped bring us together as one team. The blame game ended because everyone could now see how he or she could impact both sides. The finger pointing stopped and the engagement level went through the roof. It led to a complete culture change."

Now that they were all working for the same goals, they realized that those who had the best relationship with prospective donors were the ones who could encourage those prospective donors to make good on their pledge.

"It got rid of the mentality of 'It's not my job,'" said Katie. "It all disappeared once we started trying to hit group goals and creating the line of sight into how everyone's day-to-day actions could impact those goals. We stopped looking at each other and started looking for the 'time bandits,' the things that were stealing our time and forcing us to work harder instead of smarter. Our focus became about what we could do more of for the kids in our community."

One of the ways Katie and her team rallied around their new mission was to try to perform up to the gold standards for which the top agencies in the country were given awards. On a poster in their break room, a member of Katie's staff wrote down the performance numbers the best agencies delivered so that everyone could see what their agency was being measured against. This is not unlike how a for-profit company might benchmark itself against its competition and is one of the steps of the HIP process. Using competitive data is one of the most underutilized steps in the process. When people realize that someone else is doing better than they are, they buy into the standard set by the market. From that day on, the team owned those numbers in that they began comparing where they were and where they needed to be to achieve that same standard.

Katie and her team also realized that while the AIM system had marked them as underperformers, it could also serve as a resource for them to identify which top-performing agencies they could begin to emulate. "We were able to look at which agencies were excelling at which metrics," Katie told me, "and we started calling up and visiting with the agencies that were doing the best in the categories we needed to improve upon."

Fortunately, two of the top-performing agencies in the country were just a few hours away by car. Katie began sending her staff members on day trips to bring back tips on how they could continue to improve. The team developed a hunger to seek out answers, which was a result of them becoming engaged in the HIP process. Katie and her team even organized a regional conference with their nearby agencies so they could all gather and share their best practices.

Meanwhile, Katie and her team continued to make progress on playing the Game. The more Katie learned about it, the more intrigued she became that it could help her team find the right balance between money and mission by making decisions such as cutting expenses, raising more donations, generating new revenue-producing ideas, and, above all, helping more children.

One of the hardest conversations she had with her team concerned determining what their critical number should be, which was the one weakness in the organization that everyone could rally around. For this particular year—as mentioned earlier, critical numbers change every year—Katie and her team identified net income as their focal point. But getting to that conclusion wasn't easy, especially because some of the staff felt that Katie was prioritizing making money over helping the children in the community. Several staff members worried that programs would be cut in order to make the financial goals. But after much back and forth, Katie got the team to rally around the idea that if they didn't perform financially, they couldn't do as much good for the kids. "We had to come to an agreement about what that number would mean to the community and, for us, financial stability was essential," said Katie. "We also had to agree on what we would do with the money if we made a profit at the end of the year."

The team decided to build their growth incentive program around net income—with a catch. The team would earn their incentive bonus if they were to exceed their annual financial goals as well as their goals to serve more children than last year, which was a stretch goal since the national average number of children served per year had been decreasing for several years.

"We worked really hard by looking at the numbers to try and figure out not only how we could serve more kids, but more importantly, how we could serve the kids with higher quality," Katie told me. One of their solutions was to run a MiniGame, based on finding high-quality volunteers in the community to serve their mission.

Playing the Game over time also brought all the stakeholders together on the same page. "Our staff, donors, board members, and volunteers all have access to all of our critical numbers at any given time," said Katie. "The numbers were literally written on our walls. By providing access to the numbers and teaching those involved what the numbers meant, we were able to maximize employee engagement, board engagement, and donor engagement as a result of their input. That increased engagement was a critical component of our rapid growth."

One key ingredient of the agency's success was that the staff became extremely proficient in monitoring cash flow projections. "We began to pride ourselves on treating our agency with the same knowledge, responsibility, and business acumen that you would find in any for-profit company," said Katie.

Every staff member was responsible for weekly projections of revenue and expenses. The staff met every week to analyze the numbers and project where they would be at the end of the month, based on historical knowledge, current conditions, and aging accounts receivable. The team also reviewed the actuals and compared them with their projections from the prior month. All of the numbers were kept up to date on a scoreboard mounted in a conference room, which enabled every staff member, donor, volunteer, or board member to see how much cash was coming into and out of the organization at any given time. "Anytime that someone walked in the room, they could see at a glance the number of children we were helping, the number of volunteer inquiries, and other critical program related metrics," said Katie.

That level of engagement and knowledge also led to reduced expenses. Katie's staff began to pay more attention to costs in areas such as mileage reimbursements and office supplies. The team also ran a series of MiniGames designed to further drive fundraising while helping more kids.

By the end of that year, Katie and her team not only reached their targets but blew past them. They increased their revenue by more than 22 percent, while also expanding the number of children served by 17 percent. By making, and exceeding their goals, the team had earned the right to collect its growth incentive. The team threw a wonderful celebration at which each staff member was personally recognized and given a growth incentive check. The agency's board members were also part of the celebration, which made it even more special for Katie and her team.

"We saw such a huge transformation with every member of the staff," said Katie. "They all adopted an ownership mind-set, which proves you can get that without someone having actual equity."

The impact of playing the Game also went beyond the numbers; it built trust and camaraderie, which are essential elements, especially when something unexpected happens.

However, Katie and her team were hit by a curveball soon after that celebration, when they learned their finances were going to take a huge hit because they were denied tax credits totaling almost 10 percent of their budget. The crisis forced Katie and her team to debate their options for contingency plans. One option they debated, for example, was to leave an empty programming position unfilled. But it was a catch-22 scenario: if they saved money by not hiring the new staff member, they might not hit their targets in terms of helping children in the community.

"I realized that if I had made that decision myself in a command-and-control way it would have blown up on me," said Katie. "That would have sent the message that I don't care about the programs and that my only focus was keeping us out of the red. I needed to let the group come to a decision instead." It was a freeing moment for Katie.

After debating different options, Katie's team decided to apply for a different tax credit to offset the one they were losing. The application was massive, more than fifty pages long, but the team divvied the sections up so they could complete it together. While they waited to find out if they would receive the tax credits, the team decided to hold off on hiring the new staff member. "Everyone had a stake in that decision," said Katie. "And I didn't have to do all the work myself at midnight."

Two months later, the good news arrived: the agency got the tax credit it had applied for. The even better news was that the new amount exceeded the original amount they were denied, which put them ahead of their plan for the year.

That was another example of the hard work Katie and her team performed over a three-year period to remake their agency into a gold-standard entity among their peers.

When they finally got their metrics to that level, the team was eligible to compete for the prestigious agency of the year award, for which the winning agency would be honored by all of their hundreds of peers around the country. It was incredible that she and her associates were able to go from the bottom to being recognized as one of the top agencies in the country and Katie and her team were, admittedly, on pins and needles leading up to the national conference at which the award would be given out. Yet they knew very well what they had accomplished and they were ready to celebrate. In their refrigerator, they even kept bottles of champagne labeled, "Do not open until we win Agency of the Year."

When the big announcement was finally made—and those celebratory bottles were finally opened—Katie and her team had the honor of walking across the stage together to accept their award. "During our acceptance speech, I talked about the incredible journey we had been on with the Game," Katie told me, "and how we had fought every day to get up on this stage."

PAYING IT FORWARD

The success that Katie's agency had achieved by playing the Game created a substantial amount of interest from members of that audience and others who became interested in creating the same level of impact. "People were curious to find out more about why this nonprofit that was acting like a business was having so much success," Katie told me. In fact, the CEO of the largest agency in the country in Katie's field was so taken with Katie's story about the impact the Game had on her team that he tried to hire her, right after the conference, to implement it in his agency.

But Katie surprised him by saying that she was retiring after serving for nine years, six of them as CEO. "You're too young to retire!" the CEO told Katie. While she was stepping down from her full-time position to have more time with her young children at home, she decided to become a Great Game of Business coach and embarked on a mission to teach other nonprofits the benefits of playing the Game, beginning with helping that CEO transform his agency. She had found a way to pay it forward.

Thanks to Katie's influence, that CEO—a former venture capitalist—has already seen a transformation both in his agency and how he leads it. He was just twenty-nine years old when he took on the CEO role at a time when the agency had less than one month of operating cash. The standard was typically three to six months of cash reserves. "Being in that precarious position deeply troubled me," the CEO told Katie. "I had staff people coming to me asking when they were going to get raises, because they didn't know how much trouble we were in."

After working with Katie for a year, the CEO and his team turned around their financials while also fulfilling their mission. At the same time, the CEO reported that, thanks to the Game, he now worried about different issues than he had a year previously. "It's freed me up to think about issues at higher levels," he told Katie.

The sense of freedom that playing the Game creates can be critical since so many nonprofit leaders burn out after just a few years under the extreme burdens they take on, trying to manage finances and missions all on their own. They try to do it all and just collapse. "My graduate school thesis was about executive turnover in nonprofits," Katie told me. "I was curious what caused people to burn out. And what I learned was that many executives never learn to separate themselves and unplug from the organization. They are obsessed with their job and their missions, which leads them to micromanage everything. But the Game frees you. You don't have to be the only one worrying about the details or be paranoid that a ball is about to drop. With the Game, you become part of a team that shares that burden."

That CEO has now become a vocal proponent of the Game, which he hopes to get every agency in his organization to embrace.

Strangely enough, a key donor, an executive of a for-profit company, was so blown away when he saw their scoreboard and the dynamics of a huddle in action that he has now started to play the Game in his company. Talk about a ripple effect.

Katie's influence hasn't stopped there. She is now working with dozens of other nonprofit and for-profit organizations, getting them, too, to recognize the transformative power of playing the Game. That includes finding that balance between money and mission, but perhaps just as importantly, creating a culture in which people are truly engaged and want to work.

In her work as a coach, Katie has learned that it wasn't just her agency that struggled to attract and retain talent. The Game has become an answer to that challenge for all kinds of for-profits and nonprofits; they have come to appreciate it as a way to convey to their staff that they can build a culture that delivers on its mission without having to apologize for making money along the way. "It's all about the people," said Katie. "And if you're losing your people to your competitors and it's not just about the money, then you have to ask why you're losing them. Playing the Game provides the kind of culture and environment that people don't want to leave. They want to find ways to make a difference both in their organization and for their noble cause." In other words, Katie has been able to spread the message that you can't have values without performance, but when you have both, you create the kind of culture that can change the world.

CHAPTER NINE
THE GREAT GAME OF GOVERNMENT

C an a Great Game culture take hold in government? That was the question Tim, an elected official in a rural county, asked me once. At the time, I honestly didn't know the answer. Tim was putting together a leadership academy in his community, composed of a group of volunteers who normally didn't run in the same circles, such as the sheriff, county clerk, and members of the planning department. One of the group's main goals was to "break down the walls," as Tim put it, so that the leaders could share information and collaborate with each other. The county employed several hundred employees and worked with a budget of several million dollars, which it used for community services that ranged from law enforcement to the paving and plowing of roads. It was a complicated organization with many departments, most of which were led by an elected official with a different mission. At times, it could seem very dysfunctional; the different department heads seem to be constantly jockeying with each other for resources and attention. "We struggled to find a way to bind ourselves together as we provide a whole spectrum of almost unrelated activities," Tim told me. With Tim's guidance, this group began to meet regularly to discuss ways to improve community services.

Another goal was to get everyone to understand the county's finances. Each of the leadership academy's meetings included a brief presentation and explanation of the county's budget situation. Tim also used a newsletter as a way to report on sales tax performance every month, explaining why it was volatile and how its fluctuation affected the budget and the county's ability to give raises to public employees. "The whole dialogue between the public and the county, or any government for that matter, takes place in the wrong way," Tim told me. "Financial ignorance is a plague on our society. You can politicize ignorance. We were overwhelmed and needed more resources, and the only way to do this was to ask for a tax increase, something the public sees as just more government 'waste.'"

Tim had read about the Game and the concept of open-book management a few years back. He became interested in using the concepts of openness, engagement, and financial literacy as teaching tools for the academy, possibly as a way to find some creative solutions to budget problems the local government was struggling to work through. Specifically, the cash balance in the county's general fund was on life support. With tax increases politically unfeasible, the county was desperate for solutions.

That's when Tim posed his question to me about the Game. While I didn't know if the system would work in government, I did agree to Tim's invitation to speak to his diverse leadership group about collectively getting their budget back in shape by going beyond just thinking about their expenses. I thought I could get them to take a fresh look at taxes and how they raised revenue. I'll admit it was a strange scene to be standing in front of armed sheriffs, their pistols strapped to their ankles, talking about the Game. I wondered what might happen if I said the wrong thing.

The main point I spoke about to the group was this: the better the businesses in their area performed, and the more jobs they added and economic activity they stimulated, the more sales tax revenue would increase. That, in turn, would increase their budget and enable things such as the hiring of more police officers to address the community's security concerns. But when I asked the group how much sales revenue they would need to get their budget back in order, I got the kind of look that made me think I'd grown a third eye. I got similar reactions when I asked which industries were hiring and which ones the county earned the most revenue from. Did they collect from a wide base of companies, or was it all from big retailers such as Walmart? No one knew the answers.

I mentioned that, if I were part of their county government, I would want to know how well the companies were doing. I would want to have some idea of whether all of my eggs were in one basket. Maybe the county needed to attract companies in a variety of industries to offset seasonal or economic cycles. This is the same problem a company faces when it asks itself whether it needs to diversify its customer base. The more the county's revenue is tied to a single source, the more risk it faces.

The key point, I told them, was that the Game we played in our company involved more than openness and financial literacy; it was also about strategy, planning, and creative solutions. Why couldn't the county run a MiniGame, for instance, in which employees tried to predict what the tax revenues would be for the next quarter?

Another opportunity might be to have employees predict where the biggest revenue increase might come from, or even just who the biggest revenue producers were. The goal would be to get the county employees thinking about where the county's money came from and what could be done to encourage the people who generated it. For example, what would be wrong with sending a thank-you note to a growing business that was suddenly contributing more tax revenue to the community? Might that begin to change the way business leaders thought of elected officials? Wouldn't that be a way to begin to close the trust gap that created so much of that us-versus-them dynamic?

Let's face it. We live in an age where few of us actually trust the government, or the people who work for it. But when many of us think of the people who work for the government, we tend to focus on the folks who are elected to their positions. That might include mayors and state legislators at a local or state level all the way up to the people we see on CSPAN, such as senators, congressmen, and the president. By their very nature, these folks tend to draw plenty of attention to themselves. It's part of the job. But they aren't the only ones who work in the government offices that run our country.

There's another layer beneath the elected officials: the people who are appointed to their jobs. These are often figurehead positions where, based on loyalty or contributions to a politician, people can land a nice administrative job in the state capitol, or even in Washington, DC. The catch is that as soon as their guy or gal gets voted out, they're out of a job as well.

The people who really get overlooked, the true unsung heroes and heroines of our communities, are the public service workers who have permanent, full-time, nonelective government jobs. They're the ones who pave and plow our streets, pick up the garbage, and collect the taxes they need to pay their people to do all that work. These are the folks who watch the politicians and the appointees come and go, year after year, as they put their heads down and try to get some work done. The catch is that most of us on the outside looking in don't think they're getting much work done at all. We might even think they're doing a lousy job of spending our tax dollars. The classic image that might come to mind is that of a group of construction workers wearing neon vests and leaning on their shovels, all watching one guy who might actually be doing something. What many people consider the essence of government work—both locally and nationally is that these workers are great at wasting our hard-earned money and getting nothing done. It wouldn't occur to most people to thank any of those workers for showing up at their jobs day after day.

Now think about what it's like to be one of those government employees, especially one who works in your town. There will always be some bad apples. But there are also plenty of folks who have been drawn to public service out of a sense of civic duty or just the chance to make their community or their country a better place. But it doesn't take them long to become more jaded and cynical about their work because, regardless of what they tackle or accomplish, the public always seems to be criticizing them for what they do or don't do. I know one extremely hardworking woman, who comes home upset more days than not because she just doesn't feel appreciated for all the effort she puts into her job. She wonders all the time why she even tries, because she knows some of her colleagues don't stick their necks out as she does. She has begun to realize those folks have learned to play it safe because it never seems they can win. Someone is always going to find a way to criticize you. What makes it worse is that the departments in the bureaucracy battle each other to get access to resources and to curry favor from the elected officials and appointees. There's rarely ever a sense that everyone is working toward common goals; there's just no sense of *we*. Why has that become so prevalent these days?

What's fascinating is that the same woman told me that when someone from the community recognizes her work—or even thanks her for her efforts—she comes home on cloud nine. A single compliment can fuel her for weeks on end in dealing with the critics and cynics. That's the feeling that a winner has. The tragedy is that so many of the government workers in our country don't get the chance to win often enough.

But what if they could? Even better, wouldn't it be great if we could change the dynamic that so often seems to pit people against their government? What if people and their government—especially the true public servants who see a greater good coming from their work—were to act as partners with the shared goal of strengthening our communities? What would it be like if the people in the government were celebrated for their achievements and their hard work rather than constantly being painted as villains stealing our money? What if we were to trust each other enough to work together to overcome our challenges as communities? Is such a change even possible? It turns out the answer is yes, especially with the help of the system, which would eliminate the hidden agendas and conditions.

It's about collaboration, cooperation, and collective decision making.

I can imagine that you might be wondering what incentive a local government, or even the US Congress for that matter, might have to play the Game. Or perhaps you think governments are already open-book entities, because their budgets are public information. While that's a fair point, playing the Game isn't just about budgeting. It's about collaboration, cooperation, and collective decision making. It's about identifying critical numbers and getting everyone in an organization, top to bottom, thinking about ways to improve those numbers. So, for example, if a government were transparent with its books, it might set the debt level as a critical number and then create incentives and rewards for leaders to reduce it, either by making cuts or increasing revenue in ways that don't involve raising taxes. It's the idea that we can absorb social overhead by increasing the worker participation rate.

After my talk, Tim became excited about the idea of playing the Game in his county government. "Whether you are for-profit or not, you can't run an organization if you don't know your numbers," he said. While running a public-sector organization is very different from running a for-profit business, Tim believed they could benefit by implementing some of the Game's best practices. "Could there be a way that a citizen can see that his or her taxes are actually investments that create value?" he asked me. "Maybe if we all played a game called something like Our Town, where citizens could see the correlation between their taxes and how the programs they pay for relate directly to their home, family, or business … I would love to see our community be the best in the country at doing something like that."

A WORK IN PROGRESS

I told Tim I wanted to see that happen, too, and I would help him and his team in any way I could to get them started. Tim and I stayed in touch for several years as he tried to lay the groundwork and build some momentum in his county organization to adopt the system.

There were challenges to overcome, especially the fact that the county's leadership was composed of thirteen independently elected officials. No single person could make the decision to start playing. They didn't have one person at the top who just said, "Do this."

What they had instead was a secret weapon whose name was Cindy. Cindy was also an elected county official who had been in the audience when I gave my talk. She became a believer in the power of the system and thought it could work in government. She had also worked closely with Tim in his efforts to kick the Game off. But when Tim moved on to another job, Cindy found an opening: She had been appointed to serve as the county's interim budget director. She decided that was as good a time as any to start playing the Game. "We were in trouble and we needed a change if we were going to survive," Cindy told me. "We knew what our biggest problem was: We needed to preserve our cash."

As a first step, Cindy organized a one-day seminar at SRC headquarters to see if they could build some momentum. "We had fifty people from the county attend, which we were very pleased with," Cindy said.

She kept up the momentum from that seminar by holding the first county-wide huddle just two weeks later—this time eighteen people attended—which she treated like a budget study session. "I knew I needed to act swiftly," she told me. "Tim had done all the ground work, so all I had to do was push the train through the tunnel."

But something else also opened: Cindy began a personal transformation of her own. "I am a typical auditor," she told me. "When I started at the county, I was very shy. But as we engaged more with our colleagues and the public in our huddles, I became very outspoken. People didn't know I had that talent. I became the county's cheerleader. I became the catalyst to ignite people's fire to understand and to take action. But it was never about me or even Tim. It was about encouraging and empowering other people to step up and drive participation across different departments. What we were doing wasn't getting us there. We knew we had to change even when people don't like change. We had to get focused in moving together in a forward direction."

The team followed up that first huddle by writing an article in their monthly newsletter about what they were up to, and by holding weekly steering committee meetings. Once a month, the huddles were used to inform attendees on updates to the budget, while other huddles were used as teaching sessions. The team also began sending weekly emails to all employees that included a teaching moment from the previous week to help drive greater financial literacy and understanding of the budget.

While they had no direct control over revenue—just as many county departments do not—they did begin implementing a series of MiniGames, which were inspired by *Survivor* and *Family Feud* and in which questions involved specific facts related to the county's budget. The winning department even got to showcase a trophy, which added some friendly competition to the equation—and maybe it even had fun along the way. "Just because someone's job has nothing to do with money doesn't mean they can't solve a problem, eliminate an inefficiency, or identify a new opportunity," Cindy told me.

The team also began a game based on the notion of a job swap in which members from different departments spent a day with their peers in other areas to foster greater awareness of what each department does. That began to help break down the walls in the organization and get people to begin to acknowledge that they might actually be on the same team and working toward the same goals.

Take, for example, the story of two maintenance workers, Frank and Pete. They'd worked for the county for many years. Their role was to clean the different county buildings and make sure the different heating and cooling systems remained in working order. They took pride in their work. It used to be that when something went beyond their pay grade, they tuned out or looked the other way. There was no reward for sticking their neck out, trying to do something different—until they were transformed by the huddles.

One day, Frank and Pete were sitting in their work area, prepping for their day ahead, and they started talking about what they could do to help. They began to wonder how they could do their job differently, maybe in a way that could save the county a bunch of money. Frank pointed to the barrels of chemicals they mixed up with water to create their cleaning compounds. For years, he and Pete had just been mixing the chemicals on a one-to-one ratio with water. Neither of them had ever stopped to ask why they did it that way. "I wonder if we could use less chemicals if we diluted them with more water?" Frank asked Pete. The two of them then stooped down to read the label on the container. It turned out they could actually dilute the chemical all the way down to a six-to-one ratio with water. That meant they could use just one-sixth of the chemicals they had been using. It sounded like a workable idea, so they changed what had been considered a best practice and came up with an even better one.

Whether or not they realized the extent of their decision at the time, their willingness to find a better way to do their jobs had a major impact on the county's bottom line. Within a year of cutting back on their chemical orders, Frank and Pete had saved the county more than $10,000. How's that for the notion that small ideas and changes can add up to big time results? It all starts with giving people the chance to win, which is something that I think is so often missing for workers in the public sector.

Now wouldn't you like to think that the people working in your local government—or even the people in DC—would be trying to become better stewards of your money as Frank and Pete had for their county? At the same time, don't you think that the people working in those government agencies would like to be recognized for their creativity and dedication to making the world a better place around them? I think all of this is possible. It all comes from building trust, and crossing the trust gap that so often exists between governments and voters. To do that, we need education and transparency both inside out and outside in when it comes to our governmental organizations.

Cindy and her colleagues continue to play the Game to this day. Their weekly huddles now regularly draw more than fifty people from both in the government and the community. And the sophistication of what's discussed in those meetings has come a long way as well. "People were just reporting the budget numbers when we started," Cindy told me. "But they didn't understand them. That's changed." In fact, Cindy told me that an IT employee questioned a figure the budget office had reported—and she was right.

Cindy, whose office has been leading the charge in holding weekly financial literacy sessions for her associates in the county, said that an important lesson they remind people of is that when someone raises a question, it's about the number, not the person. There are also ample opportunities to learn the intricacies of the county's budget, since the general revenue fund is made up of more than one thousand line items.

It's about the number, not the person.

To address those communication hurdles, regular huddle attendees have stepped up to take responsibility for sharing what they learn with others in their department. The county has also implemented a dashboard with the latest numbers on its website, where anyone from the community can drill down into the financials and get the latest updates, all the way down to the county's checkbook. "It's the icing on the cake of our financial transparency," Cindy said.

BUILDING TRUST CREATES RESULTS

Perhaps one of the most lasting changes the Game has brought about in the county's offices is that the team now includes the public in its forecasting meetings. "We have improved our projections so much that we can now use them in our decision-making process," Cindy told me.

For instance, it had long been standard practice for the county to do forecasting only when it came to creating budgets for the coming year. But with the help of their new system, county officials have become apt at forecasting throughout the year as a way to make proactive rather than reactive decisions.

"I was so proud of what we accomplished in terms of our for-ward-looking projections," Cindy told me. "Learning how to do them and understand what they mean and how they affect the county as a whole has gone a long way for us to improve our decision making. It has also given us a tool to see upcoming bumps in the road in advance so that we can avoid them or mitigate the impact if we hit them. In the past, we always looked at what happened last month and last quarter. Now we are looking at what happens next month or next quarter. I was surprised at how impactful that was. I didn't realize it was like we were driving at night without our headlights on."

One of the results of this forward-looking decision making was that the county began to more accurately track where its cash reserves would be ahead of time. That was especially important to the employees, who hadn't had a raise in years. But in order to push a raise through, the county required that there be at least three months of cash reserves on hand. Normally, the actual cash reserve numbers wouldn't have been known until the books were closed at the end of the year—Hell! They weren't known at all—People didn't even realize what was needed to get a raise. That was a huge knowledge gap. But thanks to their huddles and their ability to forecast where the cash balance would be at the end of the calendar year, the county's employees were awarded their first cost-of-living raise in nearly six years, all without raising taxes. "Now we're asking questions like, 'Can we afford to replace the roof on the courthouse or prepare for a new judge?' because we're planning ahead," Cindy told me.

There has also been a cultural ripple effect in the county as well. You only have to look at the story of Frank and Pete, those two maintenance workers I wrote about earlier. They took that message to heart, as Cindy had. And the changes they and the other county employees brought about didn't go unnoticed. Based on the improvements the county had made in its cash balance—some $10 million in just five years—one of the major credit rating agencies increased the county's credit rating from a very good double-A rating to an even better triple-A. That meant that if the county ever needed to float a bond to raise money, it was now in a far stronger position to do so. When the credit rating agency asked Cindy how the county had turned its finances around in such a short period of time, she said, "It was because we played the Great Game of Government."

Apparently, there were several contributing factors that led to the increase, the most important of which was that the county's monthly budget projections were within 1 percent of actual income and expenditures. The rating agency also praised the fact that the county had adequate cash on hand to meet short-term obligations, a modest debt, and no pension liability. Rumor has it that the agency's representative, who visited the county, heard the story about the maintenance workers. He didn't believe it—at first. Then he got the chance to meet these emerging entrepreneurs in the flesh. He was completely blown away that the story was true.

In the wake of that tremendous news about the credit rating upgrade, Cindy led a huddle in which the topic was to better understand the agency's rating system and why its credit rating had been increased. That was an incredibly validating moment for the county's employees. It helped build trust within the community that the people who worked in their government, elected or otherwise, could be counted on as good stewards of their tax dollars.

Cindy, who has since been recognized nationally for her work transforming the culture in the county, admitted to me that while they have made progress as an organization, they still have room to grow, especially since many of the county's 750 employees work a second or third shift. "The task in front of us is to continue to push the game down into the organization more deeply and involve more and more employees at every level," she told me. Cindy added that the county had no intention of resting on its laurels. There was still plenty of room for improvement, which she saw as beginning with a continuation of accurately delivering departmental and office projections.

At the same time, the county undertook an even more impressive test of the trust they had begun to build with the community when they asked voters to pass a 0.5 cent increase in the county sales tax, which they would allocate to funding improvements to the county jail, as well as several other projects that had been on hold due to a lack of resources.

In the past, it would have been normal for the cynics and the skeptics to scream and holler enough to shut down that request in a minute. No one would have believed the county would use the money in the way they said they would. "At the outset, I didn't think there was a chance the voters would approve the plan," Cindy told me. "But we started educating the public before the election as a way to explain what our goals were for the money."

The election results revealed that 60 percent of voters in the community said yes to the tax increase because they *did* trust and believe the officials, which playing the Game had something to do with. Imagine if every county—or city or state or even the federal government—did something similar? Don't you think that might move the needle significantly in terms of how we view the role of government in our lives?

The county recently held an election for a new county commissioner. The winning candidate had run his campaign on the issue of financial transparency. To me, this was proof that when you raise the bottom, the top also rises.

CHAPTER TEN
OPENING UP HEALTHCARE

Years ago, I joined the board of a local hospital. The reason was simple: I wanted to learn more about controlling our healthcare costs at SRC. I figured I needed to get all the information to see where we as a company could improve. In other words, we didn't want to keep passing on costs to our associates without at least showing them we were working at slowing down the increases. In some ways, it feels as if we've been in the healthcare business for forty years. (You can read about our company's long struggles with controlling the cost of healthcare dating back to the 1990s in *The Great Game of Business.*)

In my time on the hospital board, I had numerous healthy debates with administrators and doctors about how we could better control costs, some of which led to eye-opening moments for me. For instance, a doctor told us that the best way for us to control our costs was to get our people to quit smoking. That blew me away. What that doctor was telling me was that we could take charge of our own preventative care. There were opportunities to bring the marketplace to our people and allow them to be active participants rather than just standing still and paying the bills. We had to take some of the responsibility for our impact on the costs.

While there are a lot of people who talk about bringing socialized medicine to the United States, the question of how to pay for that kind of coverage remains. The mistake many people make these days is thinking that other countries practice healthcare better than we do. That's a failure to accurately benchmark our system against the other players. The extreme cost of providing government-run healthcare has already forced the citizens of nations such as Great Britain, Norway, and even Denmark to pay more for their healthcare. Two-thirds of Canadians buy private health insurance as a supplement. Even communist China asks its people to pay up to a third of their healthcare costs out of their pockets. The challenge, it seems to me, is that we should take the initiative in keeping our costs under control rather than waiting for the government to figure things out for us.

Another thing we've learned over the years is that healthcare organizations, ranging from single doctor practices to major hospital systems, continue to struggle with balancing their operational costs against the kind of care they deliver to their communities. Even a small hospital serving a rural population can be a complex multimillion-dollar business with hundreds or even thousands of employees. Nothing happens in a hospital that doesn't touch dozens and dozens of people. Your doctor may send you to a hospital for lab testing, for example, or even straight to the emergency room. You need front-end staff to collect all the relevant information for doctors and nurses to make decisions. Then you get lab tests and radiology exams and other procedures. Then you might get admitted. Then there are respiratory therapists, pharmacists, and so on, as well as the billing staff that tries to collect payment. It's a true team effort involving potentially dozens of skilled individuals to deliver quality healthcare.

RETHINKING MANAGED CARE

Many healthcare organizations are also nonprofit entities. They operate by providing a service for the public good. But being classified as a nonprofit doesn't mean the organization doesn't make a profit. A nonprofit classification means the organization is tax exempt. Instead of having shareholders, a hospital has stakeholders in its community: earnings go right back into the hospital and the community, which needs to invest those earnings in technology, equipment, and hiring great medical staff.

But making a profit, or operating surplus, in the world of healthcare is complicated, especially these days. About 60 percent of the hospitals in the country lose money on their patient care operations: the average hospital operates with a negative 7 percent net margin. The complications relate to the cost of delivering great patient care and the cost of the insurance paying for the vast majority of that care, which will continue to spiral out of control as the population continues to age. That will put even more pressure on Medicare and Medicaid to cover those ballooning costs, which will cause them to shift more of those costs back to the hospitals trying to deliver the best care they can to their patients. It promises to become a lose-lose situation.

Hospitals are already facing the prospect that they'll be reimbursed for less than it costs them to provide medical services. And keeping track of what Medicare will reimburse is a challenge all on its own as hospitals need to decide on which of the thousands of different disease classifications a patient might fall under. To be paid, they must code their bills correctly. In an effort to modernize the system, the number of codes jumped from 17,000 to something like 144,000. Everything under the sun now has a code. A real example— no joke—is W22.02xA (walked into a lamp post). Would you believe that there is also code W22.02xD (walked into a lamp post, subsequent encounter)? How about code V91.07xA (burn due to water skis on fire, initial encounter)? You can't make this stuff up, but that's what today's hospitals have to deal with on a daily basis.

Medicare also tracks patients for thirty days after they've been discharged. If they return to the hospital within thirty days for the same condition, Medicare will only reimburse the hospital's service cost once, which makes sense to a degree. But if patients are discharged after a successful surgery and then return because they were suffering from an unrelated medical condition—for example, the results of a car crash—the hospital is still penalized. Talk about an irrational system. It's a huge challenge facing our entire society, and we need more people willing to step up with solutions to this crisis.

But we haven't been the only business that saw the potential of teaming up with healthcare organizations in an effort to solve the problem of increasing healthcare costs. The CFO of a global luggage company also joined the board of a healthcare organization in the rural South. In his position as chairman of that organization's board, he advised Alan, the hospital's CEO, as Alan struggled to balance the dynamic forces that continually reshape the medical industry, especially rural hospitals, which may often be the only healthcare provider for an entire community. The chairman, who had been practicing the Great Game system in his own business, thought that a heavy dose of entrepreneurship would stimulate all the elements to drive down costs and improve the quality of life in the hospital. He believed that a lot of inefficiencies could be rectified if everyone knew what everybody else was doing. The departments were silos and there were redundancies everywhere. They could never get ahead.

When Alan was hired as CEO in 2000, he inherited a handful of challenges, many of which he had no control over. For example, many of the doctors who saw patients in his buildings weren't employees. And yet those doctors served as the hospital's gatekeepers in that they were the ones who admitted patients and ordered tests like MRIs or x-rays.

Another challenge was that many of the people in the community where the hospital was located had no health insurance. That means that they might not always be able to afford the care the hospital was obligated to provide via its primary mission. If you go to Alan's emergency room, which is like any emergency room in the country, you will see signs on the wall, printed in two-inch black block letters on a white background, explaining that the hospital is required to provide care regardless of patients' ability to pay. "And you have to post it in a minimum of two languages," Alan told us. "So what we are saying is the service that we provide, we have to give away."

For the hospital, the catch to maintaining healthcare services was financial uncertainty: the cost of providing those services would often outstrip income. The hospital might have a supervolume month, for example, in which it should have made a $300,000 profit but wound up with a $150,000 loss instead, because the number of free-care ER visits went up 15 percent. "We have the interesting characteristic of being an industry that is both capital intensive and labor intensive," said Alan. "Most industries, or big industries, are either one or the other. We're both."

But despite these challenges, the hospital was profitable and growing after Alan came aboard—until it got hit with a double whammy in 2003.

First, their employee insurance costs doubled to more than $1 million. Then their worker's compensation carrier canceled their policy and they were forced to go into the state's high-risk pool. "On top of that, we discovered we had bad financial reporting," said Alan. "All of a sudden, we posted our first loss in quite a while and it was significant. We lost $2.8 million." Suddenly, Alan not only faced the collapse of his organization but also the possibility that his community would lose its access to healthcare. That was when Alan remembered he had a copy of *The Great Game of Business* his board chairman had given him. Its concepts had excited him. Since things were going well at the time he was absorbing the book's message, he didn't want to rock the boat. But now that the hospital was losing money, he pulled the book back off the shelf. He was ready to start playing the Game.

"It took the shot of pain to give us the courage to pull the trigger," he told me. "It was the difference between talking about a great concept and deciding to actually implement it. But when you've got a crisis, you jump in."

A TRANSFORMATIVE EFFECT

Alan set up a meeting with the board chairman and the finance committee at which he told them they weren't going to get incrementally better; they needed to do a wholesale reboot.

The first thing they decided was to overhaul their budgeting process. "Historically, we would take last year's number and add 5 percent," said Alan, "or take last year's number and add 3 percent. And then that's your number. Everybody gets their numbers, but nobody really looks at them. We decided we needed real targets. We needed aggressive targets. Targets make a difference in your business. And we're a hospital. We've had to learn this stuff from the very beginning."

Up to that point, though, the hospital's financials weren't even distributed outside board meetings and management meetings. Alan decided that had to change. "I recognized the power of overarching transparency," he said. "It's a philosophy of enlightenment. It's about ethics. The goal was to get everyone on your team financially and operationally literate, and then have them take accountability for those things."

Alan also knew he had to get the attention of the hospital's employees, especially because the management had immediately halted automatic raises. He knew he had to get ahead of what he calls the whisper game, in which one person says something to another, and that message, ultimately, gets convoluted, especially in organizations that run twenty-four hours a day. "When people don't have enough information, they make it up," said Alan. "They have answers, but they're to the wrong questions. They needed to hear all this from me, and everybody needed to hear the same message."

Alan personally met with every one of the hospital's four hundred employees over the course of thirty days, a total of fifty-seven two-hour-long orientation classes, held over a period of days, nights, and weekends. He told them they had lost a couple million dollars, and he needed their help to make money so they could stay employed and care for their patients.

"We asked every employee to attend one of those meetings," said Alan. "Everybody needed to hear. Everybody needed to know. I told them how we were going to keep score and how our hospital worked, how Medicare paid us, how an income statement works. I also introduced the idea of holding biweekly huddles to them. I walked them through it all. We came clean and explained what was wrong, how we were going to fix it, and how they would share in the rewards when we were successful." Alan also constructed a bonus plan: if the team were to reach its goals, people who had participated in the education program would be eligible for a bonus.

Even with the chance of a bonus, not everyone was interested in learning the financial side of healthcare, especially some of the nurses and laboratory technicians. "If I wanted to be a financial manager," they complained, "I would have gone to school for it. I take care of patients. I don't care about all this financial gobbledygook."

The lesson Alan was trying to teach was that the hospital first had to serve its employees well if it wanted to serve its patients well. Alan would ask the doubters, "How are you going to take care of the patients if you don't get a paycheck?" That question "opened their eyes. We built on that. People then started to realize that we had waste to cut. If you're going to build trust you have to be transparent. You just have to keep pushing information out across the whole organization."

Alan explained that by growing revenue and trimming costs, the hospital would have more resources to invest in hiring more nurses, buying better equipment, and yes, paying out a bonus.

Alan also made the point that, traditionally, the quickest path to cutting costs in a hospital was to lay people off, which he and his management team weren't going to do. "I knew what would happen to patient satisfaction and quality if we cut our staff by 20 percent," said Alan. "Longer call times, longer waits, and less attention paid to patients, all of which would lead to lower satisfactions rates. But lower satisfaction means fewer people will want to come to our hospital. And that affects your financial success because, again, you lose time with your patients, your doctors, and your staff. And you start losing people. You get that downward spiral. What we learned is that nobody ever cut their way into prosperity. You've got to invest. You've got to grow. You've got to do it in a smart way."

Alan said they did lose some people, including the CFO. "When it came down to it, he was a command-and-control manager," Alan told me. "He did not like sharing information. He thought holding on to information was power."

The hospital kicked off playing the Game by introducing biweekly huddles and putting up departmental scoreboards that tracked financial and operational performance.

"We started keeping score," said Alan. "We posted our scoreboard every day throughout the hospital. People got used to seeing our indicators, what was going on—how many patients were admitted to the hospital versus our budget, how many deliveries we had, patients in the ER cases, how many surgical operations we did, workplace safety, how many days since the last injury—which was something we had never done before. And then we started tracking how we were doing against the bonus threshold." Even better, from Alan's perspective, was that people started creating their own scoreboards, which helped build momentum as they secured some early wins. Things finally began to percolate from the bottom up.

One area they needed to improve, for instance, was the up-front collection of payments to minimize the number of patients who left without paying their bill. One of Alan's VPs suggested creating a MiniGame in which their admitting clerks could earn a bonus by politely asking patients to pay when they checked in. If the admitting clerks could collect $10,000 in a month, they would each get a $200 bonus.

At first, the clerks said they could never do it, since their current payments at check-in averaged $2,000 a month. But they made their goal. So, they were asked to do it again. And they did—for three straight months. "We then stopped the bonuses because, by then, it had become a habit," said Alan. "They had solved an important business problem."

The hospital had also been farming out about 70 percent of its receivables to a collection service that took up to 22 percent in commission. When the hospital brought receivables collection back in house, it not only added to its bottom line but also helped maintain better patient relationships because of its softer approach to the collection process.

The team even ran a MiniGame that taught their supply clerks to reduce outdated inventory, and another MiniGame that tracked how long radiology technicians took to perform a procedure, which helped to smooth out workloads. "This is not about one person," said Alan. "It's about a team. It's not a CEO, not somebody who sits in an office, but it's you out there every day talking to people, sharing the information. You're out there building trust because you're transparent with the things that make sense to the business, teaching them how the business runs."

Eventually, as the hospital prospered and grew, it ran out of space for surgeries and in-patient procedures. So, under Alan's leadership, they built an entirely new hospital, a 194,000-square-foot-facility. It was financed without any community tax support, which is unheard of in rural areas.

"In our organization, healthcare is built significantly around process and around expensive equipment," said Alan. "We have a pair of 360 slice CT scanners. You have to go to a big city or somewhere big to find those. When we put those in, we were the only hospital in the state with that technology. The more slices you have, the higher resolution, the faster the scanner, and the better the image. We are the smallest hospital in our state with an interventional cardiology program. People fly in, now, on helicopters from the EMS to our hospital so that we can do angioplasty. We can stop a heart attack, and that's in a fifty-seven-bed hospital." They also built a regional cancer center that uses expensive equipment such as a $2 million linear accelerator to help them deliver breakthrough cancer care.

With this advanced technology, Alan and his team could recruit additional staff, including twenty-nine doctors, who also brought referrals from as far as forty miles away. From the time Alan started to work there, the hospital grew from a total of 376 employees to a payroll numbering more than one thousand, all in a town with a population of less than twenty thousand people. They were creating jobs as they grew the organization.

"We continued to grow while everyone else was trimming," said Alan, who was also proud of the fact that his organization was rated as one of the top hospitals in the country for multiple years in a row, based on superior patient satisfaction grades and financial performance.

By opening up his books and teaching everyone who worked there to win together, the hospital broke through its financial and operational targets as well. Patient admissions and observations climbed from 2,700 a year in 2003 to more than 7,000 by 2013, which helped propel their top-line revenue from $91 million to $485 million, a 462 percent increase over ten years. Just as impressively, the hospital generated $20 million in EBITDA in 2013—up from $1.7 million in 2000—which helped grow its fund balance some 200 percent to more than $60 million.

"I'm the guy that's out there banging the drum all the time, saying you've got to stay liquid," said Alan. "You've got to keep your cash. I want us to continue to be good stewards in the community. We have to be careful and responsible to manage something that belongs to somebody else. We're going to leave this for the next generation. We're creating jobs. We're creating community. We're giving the opportunity for people to be great and achieve their own personal goals. That's how we're able to do more good in our community and for our people. That's how we can make a positive impact on the world, all thanks to playing the Game."

TAKING OWNERSHIP

Alan's story demonstrates that the power of the system can have a dramatic impact on containing the cost of healthcare by teaching the providers to think as businesspeople do. At the same time, our system can help organizations control their own healthcare costs, which was part of my goal in joining the board of that hospital. By bringing knowledge of how healthcare services operate to the people in our organization, we have been able to keep the costs to our associates under control for more than a decade.

While other companies try to keep their costs in check through managed care programs, we have been able to keep our costs under control by using our huddles to teach our associates about what drives up healthcare costs. Examples of this include patients not having a primary care physician and going to the emergency room instead, which increases the cost to the company threefold or fourfold. You get the kind of mind shift you need when your people think about the money the company pays for healthcare as their money rather than just as an entitlement. We pay every invoice.

As a self-insured business, we have held our healthcare costs at 40 percent below the national average. For example, while the average annual healthcare expense is about $28,000 for a family of four, our company averages less than $12,000. We benefit from some of the lowest costs in the country. It's about getting away from consumerism in healthcare, in which people don't think before they buy. In our organization, our system encourages people to think things through and take well-informed action. Now imagine what kind of ripple effect it could have on society if every organization were to use the system to control their healthcare costs as well as their other costs? It would be profound.

CHAPTER ELEVEN
A COLLABORATIVE WORK IN PROGRESS

The Great Game of Business is a work of art on which many artists have collaborated, including those of you who have just read about. We weren't working from some academic's plan. We didn't build this system in a vacuum. This was something that we were building up on our own from the ground floor of a factory. We began at the lowest of the low points imaginable. You can't get much lower than an 89-to-1 debt to equity ratio, with money borrowed at an interest rate of 18 percent. We were trying to survive. But sometimes it's the sublime and the ridiculous that become the obvious.

We thought that treating business as a game would somehow be easy. Again, we were completely naive. It was the first in a long series of what you might call oh-shit! moments. We would put something in place and, when we screwed it up, we had to figure out how to fix it. What we didn't know couldn't stop us. But that's how we evolved: one tweak at a time.

What we learned is that when you teach and share the numbers with everyone in the company, three things happen:

1. **You inspire trust and confidence.**

2. **People engage from the bottom up in creating their vision of the future.**

3. **Finally, the whole organization unites around an audacious goal or dream.**

The way we saw it was once everyone understands the rules, knows how to keep score, and has a stake in the outcome, you have to get out of the way and let the players play. People are transformed when they feel they make a difference working within a leadership system.

Our whole idea was to create this big pie of wealth and share it with the people in the organization. We wanted to create a democratic system to run the business and create wealth and then give everyone equity. We thought giving people stock was a simple idea. But we knew nothing about the obligations that come with sharing equity. We didn't know what we didn't know. We never gave any thought to the need for an exit strategy or the need to generate cash to pay stockholders. We also believed in treating everyone fairly, which is different from treating everyone equally. That was another one of those oh-shit! moments we had to find an answer for.

Now, it's one thing to say crazy things such as promising to hand out stock to everyone when you don't think anyone is paying attention, or to put a system into place when you don't have much to lose. But as we opened our books to our people, we also opened ourselves up to other companies so they could come in and poke and prod at what we were doing. We just let people—customers included—come onto our factory floors and ask any question they wanted. We opened up our culture.

Skeptical members of the media were also invited, including top-notch business journalists such as Bo Burlingham from *Inc.* magazine. Bo and his colleagues wanted to find the flaws they assumed we were hiding behind a curtain. They wanted to see where the bodies were buried. We didn't try to structure their investigations. We didn't have any curtain or secrets we were trying to hide. We said they could come in and go anywhere they wanted, keeping safety in mind, and ask anyone any questions they had. We even invited them out to the bar near the factory, Joanne's Expressway Lounge, to drink beer and shoot pool with us. We said, "Go find the warts so we can fix them." And they did find some warts. But you know what? They said, "Oh, that's normal. There's always something you can do better at." Then they started writing all these positive stories about the system, which spread like wildfire.

There were always doubters. When Bo and I wrote an article together in *Inc.*, titled "Why I Hate Being the Boss," which became part of the basis for *The Great Game of Business*, some people thought we were running a kind of hippie cult. Teaching employees how to make money and sharing ownership with them was pretty radical stuff to be writing about at that time.

The crazy thing was that when some people read the article—or the book—they wanted to do the same thing in their business. We struck a chord somewhere inside them; we touched something in their hearts. It just seemed to be the right thing to do, but they didn't see anyone else doing it. We validated that there was a better way to run a business, and they wanted to see it firsthand. Just as we were, they were also seeking something better. They were curious. And as naive as we were, we published the company's phone number in the book and invited readers to call us if they had questions.

We started getting phone calls from people who wanted to visit us in Springfield, Missouri, and see the Game in action. Since we had already embraced the notion that we were going to open up everything in the business to our people, we thought it would be cool to try and become one of the most open companies in America by opening our doors to interested visitors as well.

Boy, did they come! While that was validating to us in so many ways—people traveled from all over the world to tour our plant—it also became a distraction. The more we opened up, the more people wanted to know. I think the tipping point came when one visitor, a well-known female CEO, tucked her legs behind her head in some kind of fancy yoga pose during one of our company-wide huddles. You should have seen how wide the eyes got among the people sitting around her. Enough was enough.

That's when we decided to launch a new organization, also called the Great Game of Business, which would serve as a teaching and coaching organization. I'll admit part of our motivation for this was to get some work done on the factory floor again. More importantly, our goal was to share our successes in hopes that we could convince people of the power of what we had learned. We wanted to teach them to play the system for themselves. We also decided that if all of these people were so interested in what we were doing, maybe we could get them all together for a conference, which became the first annual Gathering of Games held in 1992.

Thousands of people representing hundreds of companies from all over the world have since attended the Gathering. It's become something of a homecoming for people, especially for those who have been playing the Great Game for decades. For them, it's a chance to catch up with old friends while also finding the sparks to trigger new ideas for keeping the Game alive and thriving in their own organizations. It's like going to a spa where you get the chance to recharge, which can be important because, I'll admit, it's not always easy to play the Game. Some days, you might be tempted to give it all up. So you should find every way you can to make playing the Game, and winning it, fun. That's how you get past the boredom and monotony that plague so many workplace cultures. It takes more than putting up posters in the break room to do that. It takes a community.

Over the years, the annual Gathering has become the focal point for that community. It has been incredibly humbling to have household names such as Southwest Airlines, Whole Foods, Patagonia, and Outback Steakhouse participate because they liked what they heard. People still remind me of the time a president of Harley-Davidson drove a motorcycle onto the main stage when he gave his talk. The noise was unbelievable. And how about the fast-food chain Chick-Fil-A? Have you ever noticed how incredibly efficient those restaurants are—and how friendly everyone seems to be? Members of their team came to the Gathering for years, not just as speakers but also as teachers who showed us that the financials can be translated by all employees, including part-time, hourly workers, while they are also learning to think and act as if they owned their workplace.

Jack Callahan, an executive at Allstate Insurance, came to the Gathering to describe how that company created software to train associates to read the numbers and play the Game. Jack explained that by sharing information and teaching people how to use it, his company was building trust and igniting passion.

These folks also came to do more than just talk and teach. They would take our ideas back home with them and adopt them in their own way. Then they'd come back to the Gathering and teach us what they had learned, which helped us evolve the system even further.

What we never completely realized was that they were proving this system works everywhere.

Stories in the media led us to be invited all over the world to share the lessons we were learning. Can you imagine what it was like to be invited to Africa to teach copper miners financial literacy, using a fifty-five-foot-high scoreboard? Or to hear that politicians in countries such as Egypt and Australia wanted to explore the benefits to their economies of opening their books and teaching financial literacy?

There was also the time when the prestigious Business Enterprise Trust, which was founded by the famed TV writer Norman Lear and James E. Burke, the former chairman and CEO of Johnson & Johnson, gave us an award. People such as Warren Buffett of Berkshire Hathaway, Katharine Graham of the Washington Post Company, and Henry Schacht of Lucent Technologies served on the board of Business Enterprise Trust, which was established as a response to Wall Street trader Ivan Boesky's infamous "Greed Is Good" speech. The idea was to award a prize to exemplary businesses. In 1993, they picked SRC.

I'll never forget walking up to the podium to accept the award when Warren Buffet stood up and handed me his wallet. He then asked me to let him be one of the first investors in our company if we ever went public. I politely gave him his wallet back and thanked him for the kind words.

But it wasn't just the big-name companies who helped push the system forward. The small and medium-size companies were the real powerhouses in adopting and evolving the system. Companies such as Zingerman's Community of Businesses and Image One from Michigan pushed us. Daryl Flood, Amy's Ice Creams, and Kiolbassa Sausage, all from Texas, took the Game and ran with it. So did Peterson Trucks and Commercial Caseworks from California; Wilder Design from Maryland; New Belgium Brewing from Colorado; Dorian Drake, a global trading company based in New York; and Wayne Automatic Sprinklers in Florida. The list goes on and on. These companies were the ones that weren't afraid to wholeheartedly embrace what we were doing and help us do it better. They still do.

We continue to run into the cynics and the skeptics who tell us that this system couldn't work in their company or their industry. There were doubters all along the way. This is only good for manufacturers, they would say. It could never work in a bank or a hospital or in government; there was no way this could work in a business with multiple locations; this couldn't possibly work in a company that employed a workforce that didn't speak English, let alone multiple languages; this might be fine for a small business but could never really work in a business the size of a Fortune 500 company. And the one thing everyone was positively sure of was that this system could never work in any union organization.

Or could it? We didn't know. We have always assumed that the critics might just have a valid point.

For example, people always ask us why this system isn't taught in business schools. We don't have the answer. Is it because it's not the product of an exhaustive academic study that would somehow validate the results? But how much more validation do you need? Every person who plays the Game is a validation of the system. It's as if people decided not to wait for the FDA to conduct its four years of trials before taking the medicine. They were willing to take the risk with their organization because, deep down, they knew it was the right thing to do.

As more and more companies began to emulate and play the system, they would tell us how it was working and that, yes, it could work in multiple locations and in different languages, and for big public companies, though they might call it something different. It works everywhere because, quite simply, we all use the same scorecard: the financial statements.

As we were writing this book, I was saddened to hear about the loss of Herb Kelleher, the founder of Southwest Airlines. I'll never forget the time back in the early 1990s, when we were invited to Texas to talk about the Great Game of Business with Herb and his team at Southwest. After I gave my talk, I figured everything I had shared about our open-book story wasn't worth much, given how big Southwest was and in how many locations the company operated. I wasn't sure our Great Game system would work in a big company.

Then Herb stood up. He took over the podium and told his leaders that there were only five things that could take out their company: their five unions. I admit I was shocked because I didn't know they were a union company. But Herb then told his team that the only way their airline would make it was by teaching everyone, all ninety thousand people—including every union employee—how the company made money and generated cash.

Just a few months later, a front-page story reported that Southwest Airlines and one of its unions had struck an unprecedented ten-year deal that excluded wage increases for several years in exchange for equity shares and profit sharing. By teaching people the business, Herb got them to understand the real wealth building opportunity was in stock options and profit sharing, not chasing higher wages.

Well, that story continues today. Every year, Southwest announces how much of its annual profits it shares with its thousands of employees, which works out to a bonus of, on average, more than 10 percent for each employee, a practice that has continued for forty-five years and counting. Imagine that: an airline that's been profitable for forty-five years. The amazing thing is that Southwest credits the Great Game for helping it to teach every employee how to watch the numbers and to have fun doing it. Ann Rhoades, an early employee of Southwest and one of the founders of Jet Blue, has been a speaker at our annual conference on several occasions. She has explained how the high-performance cultures of both airlines have been built on those principles, what those airlines call the big game.

I guess we can say that Southwest has proved that sharing a stake in the outcome can work in a union shop as well as in a big public company, right? Doesn't it make you wonder whether the critics have anything left to hold on to when someone asks why every business is not run this way?

Of course, Herb Kelleher spent his entire life proving the critics wrong, just as we have been trying to convince people that learning the basics of business, including financials, can empower them to live their version of the American dream.

CONCLUSION

SO WHY ISN'T EVERY COMPANY RUN THIS WAY?

The doubters remain even today, despite the track record of more than forty years and the thousands of companies that have embraced the system and run with it. I'm not sure what else they need to be convinced of. It's been hard for us to talk about the system and run the company at the same time for fear that if we failed, we would let down the system. After all, we live in a world where we eat our young. But even if our business were to fold tomorrow, the system will continue.

Just look at all the organizations that have adopted this system and driven changes, refinements, and improvements, over time. It is the people who come to visit us or talk to us over the phone who force us to turn left or right or climb a mountain. They are the ones who validate our system. They cheer us on. We have listened to the wisdom of the crowd. We still do.

We have honed and improved this process together because the marketplace, the community, all of the Great Game system's followers demand it from us. They are the ones who move the needle and rewrite the blueprint. They prove this system works anywhere and everywhere.

Today, as the experiment continues, the living laboratory isn't just in Springfield. This isn't the story of a single company anymore. It's about the growing community of people playing the game, literally all over the world, in every kind of industry, business, and nonprofit organization you can imagine. As I mentioned earlier, it's become a full-blown movement. As we say, it might be easy to stop one guy, but it's pretty hard to stop one hundred, or one thousand, or one million. Who knows how many people we can inspire?

The catch is that when you start a movement, the questions don't stop coming, which means you continue to hunt for the answers. Our system grew out of seeking answers to the questions our people were asking. Every time we were asked a question we didn't know the answer to, we went and found it and increased our knowledge because of it. And the more we taught people, the more they taught us. This leadership system will continue to evolve and improve, thanks to all the players.

I'll admit that the journey won't always be easy and will probably always be a work in progress, but it also offers the chance to create many happy endings. Maybe it's that sense of hope that can empower you on your own journey with the Game and help you answer why you're playing it in the first place. Maybe you're playing the Game to give people the power to chase their dreams.

Think about how most people you encounter on a daily basis don't really enjoy waking up and going to work every day, if they go at all. When many or most people reach a certain age, they find it more comforting to think ahead to retirement than focus on what they might need to do that day at work. And yet there is an associate at our company who still chooses to come to work even though he's seventy-one. His job on the factory floor pays him about $31,000 a year. He doesn't continue working for the pay; he shows up every day because he sincerely loves his job.

There's more to the story, however. This associate, Steve, has been working for our company since 1983, when we bought ourselves out from International Harvester. Steve has always been a hard worker and very quick to pick up new tasks. I'm not sure Steve had much formal education after high school, so in a lot of companies, he might have been overlooked or undervalued. But he found his place in our business, and he's flourished over the years on the job.

When I've told people this story, the first thing they ask me is why would a seventy-one-year-old keep working for $31,000 a year? Is he broke? Does he do it just for the money? Hardly. Would you believe me if I told you that since Steve became one of our employee-owners over forty years ago, his shares in our ESOP are now worth more than $1.4

> **He knew that the job had given him the opportunity to fulfill his version of the American Dream, which was to ensure that his kids would lead a better life than he did.**

million? It's true. When I asked Steve if he was planning to retire soon, he shook his head no. Steve liked his job too much to walk away. He knew that the job had given him the opportunity to fulfill his version of the American dream, which was to ensure that his kids would lead a better life than he did.

Another story that continues to stick with me involves another of our associates, a guy who also happens to be named Steve. He is an engineer who has been with our company for many years. When he turned fifty-five, he had the option, as everyone in our company does, to diversify the money he had built up in his ESOP account. The idea behind that rule is to allow employees to avoid having all their retirement eggs in one basket, which, in this case, was our company's stock. But Steve never diversified, which scared the hell out of me, especially as our stock price continued to climb. At the time, shares of our company's stock were valued at about $20. The last thing I wanted to see was that anything should happen to wipe out Steve's investment.

Every year, I would talk to him and bug him to diversify his personal balance sheet. I told him that I had diversified my own portfolio by selling back our company's stock to be redistributed to the current associates. But Steve wouldn't budge. When I asked him why he felt so confident about keeping all his money in the company's stock rather than investing some of it in the stock market, he gave me a simple answer: "Jack, I don't think I can do better by investing somewhere else. Why should I diversify when the company is already diversified?" That blew me away. He was right! Steve understood that our company had continually invested in products and new markets to ensure that all of our eggs weren't in a single basket. We were always trying to cover ourselves in case something went wrong. While I had been earning just a few percentage points on my other investments, Steve's portfolio had grown since that time by more than 20 percent a year. I started kicking myself and wondering what I had been thinking.

This, in a nutshell, shows the power of playing the Great Game of Business over the long term. This kind of thing happens all the time when you empower people with information. It's the wisdom of the crowd in action. You see it when your people understand how the business is run and what contingency plans you have built in to weather the bad times and reap the harvest in good times. "The

Game is simple: you teach the employees how they affect the business by opening the books and showing how that affects the outcome of their company, stock value in the ESOP, and pay," Steve told me. "It empowers the associates with knowledge so they know why they are doing what they are doing."

It's hard to argue with Steve's logic since our company's stock has more than tripled in value since Steve had the chance to sell off his shares. He clearly made the right decision for the right reasons. He believed he was the company. He saw how he could make a difference, and he has been able to grab the brass ring. As a result, he's now living a beautiful retirement after a thirty-five-year career.

His example also hammers home the point that the more we have taught our people, the more they have taught us.

We've been doing this at our company long enough to begin to see many of the folks who started with us retire and move on with a sizable number of zeroes in their retirement account. And it's amazing how a few of these individuals have applied the lessons they've learned over the years to their post-SRC lives in pursuit of their version of the American dream.

A few years ago, I got a phone call from Loren. He was the head of an organization that promotes employee ownership of companies as a viable path to shrink the wealth gap that exists in our society. Loren was reaching out because he knew that SRC had put access to information as well as ownership in the hands of its people from its very start as an independent organization in 1983. We completed that process in 2011, when we became 100 percent employee owned through our ESOP. We remain proud of the wealth we have helped create for our people over the years through their ESOP shares. More recently, there have been more than a few frontline hourly workers, some of whom never finished high school, who have retired as millionaires, thanks to their shares in the ESOP. But it was never just about handing stock to people. As we say in one of our company's ownership rules, "Stock is not a magic pill." The real magic is that, as part of our leadership system, we have been teaching our people, for more than forty years, how to speak the language of business through financial literacy. Thanks to playing the Game, we have built a business of people who think and act as owners do. They have learned to take control of their own destinies by diversifying SRC's lines of business and developing contingency plans that protect jobs and grow the company, over time.

That's why Loren was calling. The concept of employee ownership—specifically ESOPs—was under attack. Some powerful politicians in Washington, DC, held the view that it was too risky for employees to own a stake in the company where they worked. They thought older people would blow their retirement funds because they didn't have the financial literacy to make good decisions. There was a lot of talk about making ESOPs illegal because employees could accumulate a lot of money but not know what to do with it when they retired. Loren needed our help to fight back. We were floored by the news. We told Loren we would do anything in our power to help. "That's great," he said. "I wonder if you have any stories of your people you could share that show how their accumulated assets helped create a sense of financial security for them or that showed how feeling like an owner created a better sense of engagement with the business?" His next question resonated with me even more. "Do you have any stories you could share about how teaching people to be businesspeople has a positive ripple effect on their lives outside work?" Loren was asking us to show we could close the wealth gap by teaching people the rules of business, helping them keep score, and giving them a stake in the outcome. In other words, he was looking for stories showing how our system was helping people pursue their version of the American dream.

One example we pointed to was John, who had worked as a fuel injection operator for thirty years before retiring in 2011. He's now about seventy, but unlike most retirees, he's still running full-bore. After he retired, he started his own lawn-mowing business with seven employees and now services thirty properties. To get that business up and running, including purchasing a bunch of equipment, John used the business lessons he learned in our company. He taught his employees that same business literacy: how to understand an income statement, balance sheet, and cash-flow statement. More recently, he became the lead investor in a forty-eight-unit mobile-home property from which he'll receive rental income for years. In other words, John was diversifying his portfolio to help better protect his retirement and family.

"I could not have done any of this without the company teaching me the numbers and how to look beyond the day-to-day and into the future," John told me. "It gave me the foundation to know what to look at in terms of costs and how to manage cash flow. I'll admit I thought it was all hogwash at first. But over the years, as I saw the numbers in my ESOP statements grow, it convinced me that financial and business education works. It taught me that we could achieve a better life for ourselves. Every penny of the money I used to make that property investment came from my ESOP plan, and I know that in a few years, I'll make it all back and then some. If it wasn't for our ESOP plan, I wouldn't have the comfortable lifestyle I have today."

Then there's the example of our former associate Warren. He and his wife have dinner out on the town most Friday nights. A night out is a treat for Warren, who retired in 2006 after working thirty-one years at our company. There were many years when he didn't have the money to go out to eat at a nice place, let alone pay his rent, because he couldn't manage his money.

When he first took the job at SRC, in 1983, he thought, because he had dropped out of high school, he was lucky to land a gig paying $6 an hour. But he quickly found out that his wages didn't stretch far, especially when it came to feeding his family. It seemed no matter how hard he worked, or how many overtime shifts he volunteered for, he couldn't get ahead. It was as if his checking account had sprung some kind of leak he didn't know how to plug. It helped that his wife had a good job, which kept them afloat.

That all changed when Warren's wife was unexpectedly laid off. After that, Warren's life was like trying to hold on to a greased pole. The more the past-due bills began to pile up, the less Warren slept. He still clocked in to work every day, but he had begun to rack up a whole slew of demerits for being late and screwing up on the job. He led the company in wage garnishments. He had reached the bottom of the barrel and was close to losing the job he couldn't afford to lose.

At that time, he worked in one of our warehouses. It was his job to maintain the inventory of parts and pieces the other guys and gals on the assembly line needed to turn greasy, worn-out, combine engines into remanufactured products that we then sold to farmers.

Warren had been with the company while we were still part of Harvester, which helped breed feelings of distrust about the management of the company. Even after we had made the transition to owning the company ourselves, Warren remained a doubter. He figured we kept a set of books that was different from the one he saw. He thought we were simply doing what business leaders do: skimming plenty for ourselves. He also didn't think much of this ESOP thing. He was skeptical that the company didn't take anything out of his paycheck to give him a stake in the company. He felt that because his shares were worth so little, the whole thing was a joke.

Then, during his darkest days, something changed for Warren. As he sat in the huddle and saw his peers talking through the company's income statement, balance sheet, and cash flows, something hit him like a flash of lightning. He suddenly saw that inventory, the stuff he managed every day, was really just cash. His cash! For all those years he had been working in the warehouse, he hadn't realized that inventory was valuable, the fuel the business ran on. But if the company had too much or too little inventory, it lost cash. It was his job to find the sweet spot, the just-right amount that would propel the company like a rocket ship. And when he could do that—bam!—that number on his ESOP statement could begin to mean something special. It was a moment of transformation for Warren: he realized he could make a difference.

At that turning point in Warren's career, he began to trust. He went from doubting to leading. He transformed from being an employee to becoming an owner.

Warren also brought back home with him the skills he was acquiring in running a business. He and his wife began to put a plan together to get out of debt, using those dinner dates as meetings to go over their long-term financial plans. He even got a job at our company for his son, who still works there today.

Thanks in part to his shares in the ESOP, Warren was able to retire debt-free when he turned sixty-five. Soon to turn eighty, he now lives with his wife in a nice home on five acres they own outright.

While they could certainly afford to go out to eat every day of the week, Warren and his wife keep it to once a week. They remember what it was like to go hungry. They also still make the most of their time by treating their night out as a huddle, a chance to go over their budget and forecast their week ahead. Apparently, old habits die hard.

But that's not all. Even after he stopped working, something about the Game stuck to Warren like an itch he couldn't scratch. This system had changed his life; it had saved him. He wanted to find a way to pay it forward. So he did.

Warren went back to school to become a certified credit counselor. When I learned about this, I couldn't believe it. After all, this was the guy who was always out of money. But when I asked him if he was kidding me, Warren put me right in my place. "Who better than me to teach these lessons?" he asked me. He was right. He had learned the hard way to climb out of debt, which he could turn into a powerful case for avoiding debt in the first place. Debt is the ugliest place to be in, no matter if you are a young person in college or an older person trying to enjoy the golden years of retirement.

As a certified credit counselor, Warren now helps folks balance their own budgets and understand what they need to do to own a house of their own. He teaches up to four hundred couples a year to build scorecards and track their progress on achieving the same kind of financial freedom he earned, thanks to deciphering the secrets of building a great business.

"One of the key lessons we learned on the job by playing the Game was to identify and prioritize our weaknesses and improve upon them," Warren told me. "Every year we would create a bonus plan around our biggest weakness. Eventually I realized that those lessons also applied to my personal life. Once I learned the basics of monitoring the income that was coming in compared to what was going out, to watch the ebb and flow of the money, it changed everything for me. It allowed me to come up with a plan and to execute on it.

"When I got my first ESOP statement, it had probably 50 cents in it. But toward the end, it was incredible. The money from the ESOP helped me build up my counseling business into a lucrative living. I make more money now than I did when I was working! The lessons I learned at SRC allowed me to go to another level. It's an incredible opportunity for a working person to take himself to another level that he will benefit from for the rest of his life. I finally found freedom."

It's worth noting that Steve, John, and Warren all spent their careers working on the front lines for a living wage. But they took advantage of our bonus programs, 401(k), and ESOP, to save the kind of money they needed to retire. Just as importantly, they learned how to take short-term gains from funds such as their wages and bonuses and turn them into long-term investments. They went beyond their jobs to create more jobs and wealth for others, which demonstrates the transformational power that this institution we have built together can have on our communities. These are all Horatio Alger stories of regular folks making their dreams come true. The impact extends way beyond our day-to-day working lives. It's a way to take a step toward fulfilling your own version of the American dream. It has a snowball effect that is truly changing lives all the way down the line—and it's still rolling.

As I look back on the legacy of what we started at SRC with the Game, I am most proud of those transformation stories about people such as Steve, John, and Warren, who reached up to grab the brass ring of opportunity. But that journey isn't over. A lot of people might read about the Great Game of Business and figure that everyone in our company is an expert because we've been playing the Game for so long. The truth is that we're all constantly learning to play the Game better every day. It never stops. You can't set it and forget it. We're now faced with teaching a new generation of associates how they can make a difference in their lives and the lives of those around them. As these veteran players of playing the Game retire, we're already training our next generation of associates: something like 45 percent of our 1,650 workers have now been with our company for less than three years. The great news is that these young people have taken to the Game like fish to water. The idea that they can see how they make a difference in their work and that nothing is hidden from them has created an incredible amount of excitement and engagement in the business. It's why the Game remains the beating heart at the center of our company's culture. It's become an engine for us to recruit incredibly talented young people to join our business, while also grooming them to become the leaders not just of tomorrow but of today.

What's also remarkable is how sticky the Game becomes for people who learn it. While companies have long struggled to attract and retain top talent, the system becomes a magnet that draws them near. A transformation occurs when something inside you is opened up and you just can't put it back inside again. All of us can create change on our own; we don't have to wait to get permission. We've had dozens of cases in which associates have left our business to work elsewhere, only to realize that once they get used to having transparency and making important decisions for themselves, they want to come back to work for us. At the same time, we've seen others leave to start new businesses, armed with the knowledge they gained from playing the Game, which is something we celebrate, sometimes to the point of investing in these new businesses.

There are also times when life intervenes in such a way that an associate really does need to move on. And this transformation goes with them. One of my favorite examples is a young woman named Rinnie, who started at our company as an intern in 2013. A relative of hers worked for us and recommended that Rinnie apply for an internship with us. She admitted she didn't know a lot about business at the time. She had completed several other internships while she was in college and knew what she was looking for when it came time for her to find a full-time job. More than pay, she wanted to work for a company that took care of its employees.

"I didn't expect very much," Rinnie told me. On her second day of work, she was in a staff meeting where everyone was clapping and cheering about maxing out their fourth-quarter bonus. She didn't know what that was. Then she started financial literacy training and other programs taught by the team at our training and coaching organization, the Great Game of Business, which continues to teach the Game to every new person who joins our organization. Rinnie remembers the teacher telling the class that the lessons they were learning could also work at home and in the community. Rinnie had the opportunity to listen to an employee named Sharon tell her story. Sharon had worked for the company for about twenty years as a maintenance worker, which is about as much of a frontline job as you can have. But thanks to the knowledge she gained on the job, Sharon had been able to pay off all her debt, including her mortgage, and was proud to owe nothing to anybody.

"That inspired me," said Rinnie. "I was twenty-two years old and didn't have a lot of responsibility. But I decided I wanted to buy a house of my own. I started playing a game at home, in February, to save enough money for my down payment. By June, I had made my goal and was able to buy a home of my own without any help from anyone else. A lot of people can't say that."

Rinnie admitted she might not have done it if she hadn't learned the power of setting and achieving goals. It also clicked for her that this was how business worked as well. "I knew we had a critical number at work where we have more than one thousand people working toward fixing the same weakness," she said. "The experience of buying a house helped me to really think like an owner because now I was one."

Rinnie told me that she continues to bring the things she has learned on the job back home with her. She's still in her twenties, but she is also now happily married with a toddler-aged daughter. She and her husband love to compete against each other to see which one of them can pay off more student loan and mortgage debt each month, something they've made huge progress on. Rinnie even has a five-year forecast to track, every month, the debt payments and progress she and her husband make toward their goals. "We are on the same team, and it's made our marriage happier as well," she said. "Thanks to using the system, we have a calendar hanging in our house that has all of our big bills posted on it. We don't keep it a secret from anyone who visits us. In a world where ignoring debt is so popular, I challenge anyone to face debt head on, make a goal, and break it!"

Rinnie said the biggest win she and her husband experienced was when they were able to adopt their daughter and cover most of the $40,000 in adoption fees without getting into debt. Few families can say that.

Because of her husband's job, Rinnie eventually had to leave SRC. They moved away from Springfield to another midwestern city. Rinnie knew she couldn't work for a traditional command-and-control business again and had to find an employer who believed in principles similar to those of SRC. Fortunately, she was able to land a new job with a roofing company whose owner believed in openness and financial transparency and gave his employees the opportunity to invest in the business. "He has a culture that is similar to SRC," said Rinnie. "One of my goals is to take what I have learned and use it to teach him and my coworkers about the Game."

The owner hired Rinnie after a Skype interview. She asked him questions such as, "What's your hairy audacious goal?" and "Where do you see yourself in five to ten years?" Rinnie was trying to figure out what kind of game the owner was playing. He was surprised she was asking him these questions.

"These are the thoughts that keep me up at night," he told her.

"He told me he wasn't used to people coming in and asking him big-picture questions," said Rinnie. "He was thrown off by why I would want to ask questions like that. I told him that I was an owner of my business, that we all owned the business. I told him I could never get rid of that mentality of being an owner. I told him that I would continually challenge him about how he can give employees a stake in the outcome to help them grow the business."

I love the fact that Rinnie's questions got to the owner; he could see that she looked at the business as more than just a job. It was clear he was excited to see that hiring someone like her could make a difference in his business. Rinnie told me she has accomplished a lot at her new job, but she's not done. In fact, at the time I was writing this, she was applying to a PhD program in business. "I will say that venturing outside SRC has opened my eyes to what I have learned," said Rinnie. "I truly believe that what the Game does on a daily basis will become the standard for the next generation. This is what the future of business will look like. In ten years, it will be the closed-book, top-down companies that will be in the minority. The next generation just won't allow it."

Let's hope Rinnie is right.

I share these stories to help make the point that the results of playing the Great Game of Business system go beyond the bottom line. The real impact is on the quality of life people are creating for themselves, giving them the opportunity to fulfill their dreams, whatever they might be: owning a home, raising a family, getting a college education without drowning in debt, starting a business, finding ways to give back to the community, or making sure their kids lead a better life than they did. The system supports the kinds of dreams that really grab the heart.

A CONVERSATION WITH A DOUBTER

We believe that by opening up our business and empowering everyone in our organization to have a say in how we approach the future, we have found a way to deal with the risk of operating a business while sharing the rewards that come with success. Our goal all along has been to improve people's well-being so everyone can flourish and prosper.

That's why, in writing this book, I'm hoping to give a little push to those of you sitting on the fence, those of you wondering what might happen if you, too, were to commit to transforming your business. For it's my belief that when all is said and done, most business owners will agree the Great Game of Business leadership system can make sense for their organization, no matter how they share a stake in the outcome.

But to be honest, I still write off the skeptics, figuring that no matter how many stories I share, they will always find some reason to keep their books closed and their people in the dark.

Believe me, I've had countless conversations over the years with doubters, people who can find every excuse for why this system won't work in their business. They are often sharp businesspeople. They just don't see how this system can make them even better at what they do.

At the same time, there's often a list of common barriers the doubters share, a list of reasons to punt on making any big changes in their business.

I remember a conversation I had with one such doubter, a sharp entrepreneur named Jay. I gave him the chance to tell me why the system wouldn't work in his business.

"First off," Jay said, "I started my business by myself with my own money. And I learned from my parents, who learned from their immigrant parents to hold information close to the vest, to not tell anyone anything, especially about how much money I was making. So, when it comes to opening my business up, I'll admit I am really uncomfortable with the idea that my employees will find out how much money I make. It's like instead of a fear of the unknown, I have a fear of the known."

This question has come up a lot over the years. My answer to Jay was that we have never shared salary information at SRC, and we don't encourage others to do it. We simply show those numbers as a summary of direct labor costs and expenses. But I also told him he was right: if he didn't want to share his numbers, or he was afraid of the skeletons in his closet, this system won't work for him.

"That helps," Jay said. "But unlike you, I'm the sole owner of my business. Even if we don't disclose individual salaries, my employees will still equate how much money the business makes with how much I'm bringing home. I think they all believe I'm making a fortune as it is."

I pointed out to Jay that employees often assume that the owners of a business are making more than they really are. They don't understand the liabilities the owner takes on and what happens when a business—God forbid!—loses money. I also think some owners harbor hard feelings toward employees they suspect don't appreciate how much the owner has at stake, something that creates an unhealthy separation in a business and can even stunt its growth. Companies can be destroyed from within by keeping too many secrets or by losing their moral compass. If you, as a leader, don't have trust, you don't have anything.

When you share information with the employees, though, you can teach them not only how to make money but also where the money goes. I reminded Jay that he had taken on debt to build his business, something that affects his cash flow in a big way. And unless he explains that debt, his employees might not understand how it affects what he takes home. It is possible, of course, for a company to be outrageously profitable and still have no cash.

"I like it," he said. "I have some employees who want me to open another store, something I would have to finance out of my pocket. Well, if I did, and it lost money, I could show them why they wouldn't be earning a bonus. That might make them think differently."

"That's right," I said. "Plus, when you begin to trust your employees by sharing the information with them, good and bad, it's amazing how freeing it becomes. You don't have to lose sleep every night worrying about having the right answers, because your employees will begin to provide some of those solutions."

"Well, here's my second problem," Jay said. "I run a convoluted business that involves people working on everything from making products to making repairs to moving boxes on a loading dock. How can I create an incentive program that won't cause people to say,

'Hey, that guy has an easier job than me. It's harder for me to hit my numbers.' I guess, to say it another way, what would happen if one part of the company got a bonus and another didn't?"

I told Jay that everyone in one of SRC's subsidiaries is enrolled in the same bonus structure. The key is that if anyone at the company gets a bonus, everyone gets it.

"That makes a lot of sense," said Jay. "But wouldn't giving my hourly employees a smaller percentage bonus cause some problems?"

I told Jay that there is no one-size-fits-all policy when it comes to bonus plans. Business owners can structure their plans in ways that make sense for their companies. But at SRC, we assign different bonus percentages to different groups of workers to encourage a desire for promotion. The differences in bonus percentages act as an incentive for folks to do better for themselves.

"Interesting," Jay said. "I guess that brings me to my third concern, then, which is, Can my employees handle the truth? What if one day, for example, we lose money? Will everyone just freak out?"

Transparency is about teaching people how to succeed. I told Jay I have always believed employees can read the truth in your face. They know. It's funny, because I hear this concern a lot. One guy told me that if he showed his people the numbers, they would leave. So he only told them the good news. I asked him if they believed him. "Not really," he said. Employees know before anyone when the business starts to slow down, only they often think it's worse than reality. They'll come up with the wrong answers if you don't tell them the truth.

Jay told me he'd never really thought about it that way before. "My whole thing was grappling with how to do this," he said. "I guess I never asked the right questions before. Now that I believe that playing the Game can help me make more money and also allow me to pay my people more money and make for a healthier company, I'm kicking myself for not doing it sooner."

What's interesting is that soon after our conversation, Jay ran into the challenge of telling his employees that they weren't going to get raises—again—after several years without one. No doubt, if he had opened up his business before then, his employees would have had a better understanding of why he had to make that decision.

Let's address that question again: If this system is so great, why isn't every company run this way? My reply might be that it all starts with you-gotta-wanna.

CHANGE THE GAME

It's Money. It's People. It's Both.

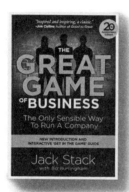
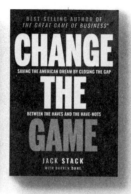
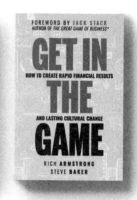

THE "WHAT"

The Origin Story of Open-Book Management

The Great Game of Business started a business revolution by introducing the world to open-book management, a new way of running a business that creates unprecedented profit and employee engagement.

Paperback: $18.95
Audiobook: $19.99

THE "WHY"

Closing the Gap Between the Haves & Have-Nots

Change the Game is an inspiration, brimming with case studies of enlightened capitalism and transformed lives, proving that business is truly the catalyst for lasting change in the world. This powerful book explores the impact of business and financially literate population in every sector

Hardcover: $29.95
Audiobook: $19.99

THE "HOW"

The Definitive Guide on Implementing the Great Game of Business

Get in the Game is a practical guide to create rapid financial results and cultural change. It outlines the 10 Steps of Implementation with case studies from real practitioners, with all the tools, tips, and hacks that our Coaches use to implement The Game.

Hardcover: $29.99
Audiobook: $19.99

HOW WE HELP

Talk with a Coach

There is no quicker, more effective way to implement The Great Game of Business than with the help of a practitioner: someone who's lived it. Our goal is to give you the tools, information and understanding necessary to be successful. To provide you with the support and extra attention you deserve, our practitioner coaches have the experience and savvy to give you the hands-on approach you're looking for and help you achieve your objectives as quickly as possible. We are happy to provide you with a complimentary thirty-minute coaching session with one of our practitioner coaches to help you start your journey. Visit www.greatgame.com/getinthegame to schedule today.

Workshops, Training, and Products

For nearly forty years, people have been visiting Springfield, Missouri, to see the "Living Lab" that Jack Stack founded, in the form of SRC Holdings. Today, we continue to host numerous workshops throughout the year, both in Springfield and around the world. Learn more about our workshops, training and products at www.greatgame.com.

Attend the Annual Conference on Open-Book Management

The Gathering of Games: For nearly thirty years, the OBM Community has converged to learn, share, and celebrate the practice of the Great Game of Business. Check our website for the latest locations and schedule.

Our Committed Team

Call us. We are passionate about transforming businesses and people. We practice what we preach and are here to help. You can reach us at www.greatgame.com/getinthegame, or call 800-386-2752.

Now that you're a part of the community, you have a responsibility to engage your people, be wildly successful, and share your experience with the rest of us. We want to hear your story!

Become a Coach: If The Game has had an impact on your life, and you are ready to help others take their people and organizations to before unimagined levels of success, consider joining our community of GGOB Coaching. Contact us at www.greatgame.com and click on Become a Coach. Help us transform lives and change the world!

Become a Coach

If The Game has had an impact on your life, and you are ready to help others take their people and organizations to before unimagined levels of success, consider joining our Community of GGOB Coaching. Contact us at www.greatgame.com and click on "Become a Coach." Help us transform lives and change the world!

ACKNOWLEDGMENTS

We have so much appreciation for everyone who has helped us on this journey. Thank you for letting us stand on your shoulders. It is you who have helped give us hope that a more prosperous and brighter future is achievable. You've turned on the light bulb that shows how many possibilities lie ahead of us.

Thanks also to those of you who shared your stories with us: Rob, Adam, and Becky; Ron; Sam and Jesse; Kristin, Drake, Josh, and Chris; Dave; Beth and Lorianne; Katie; Cindy; and Alan. Thanks to our collaborators who provided their valuable and thoughtful feedback: Tim, Betsy, Ryan, Bo, Krisi, and Ron.

And we couldn't have gotten this special edition into anyone's hands without the help of the team at Advantage Media who made this happen on a tight deadline.

ABOUT THE AUTHORS

JACK STACK
President and Chief Executive Officer, SRC Holdings Corporation

John P. (Jack) Stack is president and CEO of SRC Holdings Corporation. SRC remanufactures gasoline and diesel engines for the automotive and off-highway markets, distributes engine kits, manufactures power units and remanufactures electrical components, and conducts seminars and training programs specializing in all aspects of teaching people how to implement open-book management. SRC has annual sales of over $600 million and currently employs more than 1,600 people.

Stack, a graduate of Elmhurst College, came to SRC in 1979 as the Plant Manager of International Harvester after eleven years of direct supply chain management experience. In 1983, Stack and the SRC employees bought the company from IH and have turned it into what *Inc.* magazine has proclaimed "one of America's most competitive small companies." He is the author of the book *The Great Game of Business*, published in 1992, which was selected one of the thirty best business books of the year by Soundview Executive Book Summaries. This open-book management program has been recognized by the CBS program *Eye on America* and PBS's *McNeil-Lehrer Report* and has received both the National Business Ethics Award and the Business Enterprise Trust Award. SRC was also selected as one of the Top 100 Companies to Work for in America. Jack's second book, *A Stake in the Outcome*, was published in March 2002.

Jack has been named the Springfield Area Chamber of Commerce's "Springfieldian of the Year," an honor bestowed annually on a local community member who has worked to improve the quality of life in Springfield. He has also received the Springfield Business Journal's Economic Impact "Lifetime Achievement" award for outstanding professional accomplishments and contributions in the business community. *Inc.* magazine has called him the "smartest strategist in America" and named him one of twenty-five entrepreneurs selected to represent the twenty-five years *Inc.* has been published. Jack was also listed among the "Top 10 Minds in Small Business" in *Fortune Small Business* magazine. He was recently named the Remanufacturer of the Year by *ReMaTecNews* at their annual conference.

Jack serves as a director on the boards of several SRC-affiliated companies, including Newstream Enterprises, CNH Reman, and SRC of Lexington. He is a trustee for SRC's employee stock ownership program, VEBA Trust, and 401(k) Program. He also serves on the board of directors of Paul Mueller Company, and is an advisory board member of the Greater Ozarks Centers for Advanced Professional Studies (GO-CAPS), which includes Springfield and twenty of the surrounding school districts. GO-CAPS, a program for high school juniors and seniors, gives students the chance to explore their interests in engineering and manufacturing, entrepreneurship, medicine and healthcare, and IT and software solutions. Jack is presently serving as a director of Care to Learn, a local not-for-profit agency that provides relief to children with emergent hunger, health, and hygiene needs. He serves as the chairman of the advisory board of Harmony House I-Care, a not-for-profit organization that provides shelter, advocacy, and education to survivors of domestic violence. Jack is the founder of the Boys and Girls Clubs' "Invest to Invest Club," which was created in order to generate a new source of funds for their youth programs and to serve as a tool to teach business basics to club members and provide a friendly and competitive venue for the Invest to Invest group members.

Jack has been married to Betsy for forty-seven years and is the father of five children and grandfather of ten.

DARREN DAHL
Coauthor

Darren is an experienced ghostwriter and business journalist. He's written many words in his career, more than one million of them, targeting various topics in the worlds of business and entrepreneurship. That spans the more than five hundred articles he has written for publications like the *New York Times*, *Inc.*, *Forbes*, the *Huffington Post*, and *American Express OPEN Forum*. He is particularly passionate about projects that connect to the notion that conscious businesses can be a force for good and positive change in the world.

Darren has worked with some of our era's leading entrepreneurs and business thought leaders in writing blogs and white papers covering a slew of topics ranging from practical how-to pieces to in-depth profiles on some of the world's most intriguing companies and entrepreneurs. He's also ghostwritten multiple books, two of which have landed on multiple best-seller lists while others have garnered attention and applause from other leading business publications, such as the *Harvard Business Review*, the *Wall Street Journal*, and *Strategy + Business*.

Darren earned a master of arts degree in journalism from Columbia University, a master of business administration from the University of Albany, and a bachelor's degree in English and economics from Union College. He lives in Asheville, North Carolina, with his wife, Stephanie.